T3-BLC-264

12

To Linda,
This author
is a good friend
of Carol Peck of Good
News Café.

Pam -2009-

Glorious Soups
for entertaining

Glorious Soups
for entertaining

Colette Gouvion
Arlette Sirot

photographs Dorian Shaw
illustrations and styling Claire Connan

ici
la
PRESS

English translation rights © 2002 by Ici La Press

Copyright © 2000 Éditions du Rouergue

Photographs by Dorian Shaw
Illustrations by Claire Connan

All rights reserved. No part of this book may be reproduced
or transmitted in any form or by any means, electronic or
mechanical, including photocopying, recording, or by
any information storage and retrieval system, without
permission in writing from the publisher.

Published by Ici La Press
694 Main St. South
Woodbury, CT 06798
www.icilapress.com

Printed in Singapore by Imago

ISBN 1-931605-06-8

INSPIRATIONS

Cooking is both an art and an activity. Great chefs are artists who actually create recipes, come up with original combinations, and continually search to enrich their menu with their finely tuned new discoveries. Those who appreciate the innovations of the great chefs love good food, and delight in dipping into the vast reservoir of classic recipes. They may use these recipes essentially as presented, or reorganize them—sometimes adding their own innovative details. I belong to the latter group.

I have always been fond of good food and I like to delight my friends with excellent meals. That is how, one day, I became a restaurant owner. I came to adore this profession chiefly by making soups a centerpiece in my menus. Honesty, however, requires me to make it clear that the soups I chose and cooked for this book are not the fruit of my culinary imagination. In truth, I owe them to the blending of a number of sources. The countless cookbooks from around the world that I have read (as others read novels) and still immensely enjoy, the magazines that I collect, the discoveries that I made while a restaurant owner, and the chefs I have worked with, have all contributed to my recipes. I have of course interpreted, modified this or that detail, innovated, but in the end I would be unable to know now (as do most cookbook authors, except special cases) what belongs to the core of my cuisine—to distinguish between that which I unconsciously adopted from various chefs, what I used from the peasant repertoire, or what I really invented.

Therefore, I wish to thank all those who were my inspiration. I hope that the readers of this book take their turn in making the recipes their own, changing them as they please—perpetuating this cuisine that is forever recreated throughout the years and even centuries, providing an inexhaustible source of pleasure.

Arlette Sirot

THE PLEASURE OF SOUPS

Soup for dinner. The idea is neither new nor original. Most of our ancestors, farmers and workers, fed themselves with soup for centuries. Only the mighty saw an array of dishes served on their table. The more humble ordinarily had porridge, panada, and a slice of bread soaked in a bouillon which was enriched to some degree with bacon, meat, or eggs. For these vital soups we want to offer a lineage by recounting the recipes here. None of these delightful, more or less sophisticated liquids are intended as dinner starters, but rather as whole meals, meant to satisfy someone's hunger while enchanting the palate.

We concocted a list of families. You may choose from them according to circumstances, season, mood, and craving. *Invigorating* soups made with meat, vegetables, grain, etc., are the kind that satisfies the most famished. *Euphoriant* soups are consecrated to the peasant custom of *chabrot*—the dash of red wine that changes everything—but also may get their flavor from beer, white wine, or a drop of marc brandy. *Vegetable* soups are dedicated to lovers of all kinds of vegetables and even of wild herbs. *Refreshing* soups are to be served cold on a pleasant summer night. The *elegant* ones are meant for the evenings when one has decided to put out a marvelous spread. Finally, the *sweet* ones are for dessert, or exceptional snacks for friends that come by after dinner. All, except to some extent the soups of the latter category, are served with an assortment of accompaniments, or various breads, so that they make wonderfully balanced dishes.

These one-pot soup meals have multiple advantages. Nearly all of them are so easy to prepare successfully that even a child could make them. In general, soups do not require a great deal of preparation to get started, even if the cooking time, although this is not always the case, requires somewhat more patience. Except for the elegant ones, their ingredients are generally economical, and their quality–price ratio is second to none. They require only the most common set of pots. Almost all of them may be prepared ahead of time and heated up at the last moment. Soup, salad, cheese, and dessert to finish— no last minute rush, no stressed cook when it's time to be seated at the table. The host may serenely join the guests and will not have to leave them during the whole meal. Finally, the diversity of colors, textures, and small accompaniments enable the host to have great fun setting the table with interesting dishes, vegetable decoration as it was done during the Renaissance (notably with artichokes), cheerful tablecloths and a beautiful harmony of colors.

You may be concerned with the following questions: Are these "soup" or "*potage*" recipes, and what is the real difference between the two? It is a scholar's matter that is not very clear, which subsequently became more complicated under the influence of trends and as recipes became more sophisticated.

Chronologically, according to historians, *potage* wins with respect to age, since from the moment there was "pot," there was "*potage*," to designate something that was cooking in this brilliant invention of prehistoric humans. This takes us back to the Fire Age. According to results from archeological digs, corroborated by comparisons with the practice of ethnic groups that were unidentified until recently, cooking by boiling did not even wait for the pot. A rock cavity filled with water stood in lieu of the stockpot. White-hot stones or pebbles would be immersed into it and this was sufficient to ensure and maintain boiling for the time necessary to cook wild harvests. Our modern electric kettles are ultimately just descendants of this simple and judicious system. Then came pottery, followed by the Metal Age—the pot was established and is still with us today.

For the name "soup," it is another story. The word is of Frankish origin and is found in low Latin as "*sappa*," which means "to soak." What was soaked? Grains prepared as porridge, bread, and cakes. All these appeared only with the first grain cultivation, thus, after the first pot cooking. "Soup" appears in written works at the end of the 12th century, while "*potage*" is found for the first time only one century later. All things considered, it is a tie game—their similarities being all the greater since, for a long time, "soup" and "*potage*" strictly designated the same food styles. It is only in the 17th century that fashionable society, probably considering the simple soup where the bread was "soaked" too plebeian, preferred the word "*potage*," believed to be more elegant. In affluent homes, there was thus, notably at court, the *potage* course: generally four different *potages*, one more refined than the other, served in bowls, with a nice custom, the *"dormant,"* a kind of tiered tray on which spices and condiments that accompanied the whole meal were arranged. Meanwhile, the good lower classes continued for more than two centuries to feed themselves by soaking their bread in their soups to which they simply added a piece of cured pork belly, a bone, or some meat on good days.

As for us, we preferred soup to *potage*. When one says, *"À la soupe!"* (Chow time!), the colloquial, easy-going, cordial call is understood by both children and adults alike; used in both town and country, it has not changed in centuries. In this expression, "soup" is simultaneously the name of a specific preparation and a generic term with a much broader meaning of food, gathering around a table, and conviviality that is used even when there is no soup on the menu. Soup—like the bread that soaks in it, which has as many common expressions as the latter—is characterized as a powerful symbol. Since the first prehistoric porridge, it symbolizes food and abundance. Cooked by the most anonymous of women or by a great chef, it always generates a feeling of maternal, tender affection. Entertaining with soup means to give warmth to the hearts and bodies of loved ones. While making life simpler, it enables one to simultaneously celebrate love of food, generosity, and conviviality. So, *à la soupe!* Bon appétit!

Colette Gouvion

THE RECIPES

REFRESHING SOUPS

CHILLED CUCUMBER SOUP, **30**

CUCUMBER GAZPACHO, **32**

MELON SOUP WITH SPICES AND HAM, **33**

COLD BEET SOUP AND SMASHED POTATOES, **34**

CHILLED TOMATO SOUP WITH HERBS, **36**

AVOCADO GAZPACHO, **38**

TOMATO GAZPACHO AND BASIL *PALMIERS*, **40**

ELEGANT SOUPS

EUPHORIANT SOUPS

VEGETABLE SOUPS

BREAD AND OILS

REFRESHING SOUPS

Potage for hot days? Of course—if it is to be eaten cold or even chilled. A late addition to our gastronomic customs, it is an important addition and seen as adding an original touch—although quite traditional in the Iberian countries. Here we have the freshest and most refreshing recipes. Serve them with intricately, amusingly shaped breads, thanks to our cake and bread recipes (pages 82–85). Serve a dish in aspic, with a good salad, and, since everything may be prepared ahead of time, on nice summer eves you will be able to entertain without having to leave the dining table. Last detail: As colorful as they are flavorful, these refreshing soups lend themselves to all decorative fantasies. Now is the time to take out the unusual tablecloths, fun napkins, humorous glassware— and why not plastic bowls, plates, and small cups in fluorescent colors, and porridge bowls for small children.

CHILLED CUCUMBER SOUP

Le potage glacé au concombre

New flavors for conventional products. Delicately refined, if one is thirsty, this soup is thirst quenching. If one is hungry, this soup is nutritious. It is elegant and pleasantly surprising. Serve it with shrimp fritters.

Serves 4

●

Peel the cucumbers. Reserve a few slices for garnishing. Grate or very thinly slice the remainder. Place the cucumbers in a colander, sprinkle with salt, and let them rest for one hour to remove some of their water. Then mix the cucumber with the yogurt, white wine, lemon juice, onion, garlic, sugar, salt, and pepper. Cover and place in the refrigerator at least 2 hours.

Meanwhile, clean the watercress.

Serve with a few cucumber slices, watercress leaves, and the homemade shrimp fritters. Just dip the shelled large shrimp into the batter (prepared with the flour, milk, 1 tsp. of oil, and salt), carefully drop them into hot frying oil, remove when golden brown, and lay them on paper towels. Serve these fritters hot in a large serving dish where guests can help themselves.

Mint leaves may be a substitute for watercress.

Degree of difficulty: Easy
Preparation time: (15 minutes preparation 4 hours before serving. Plus 15 minutes at the last moment to prepare the fritters.

Kitchen utensils:
Grater
Colander
Large strainer
Large glass-serving dish
Deep fryer or pot for the fritters

Ingredients:
2 medium cucumbers
2 cups (500 g) plain yogurt
1 cup white wine
1 small white onion, sliced thin
1 garlic clove, chopped
1 tsp. sugar
1 bunch watercress, small
Juice of ½ lemon
Salt and pepper
For the shrimp fritters
At least a dozen large shrimp
1⅔ cups (250g) flour
2 cups (½ l) milk
2 eggs
1 tsp. oil
1 pinch of salt
Oil for frying

CUCUMBER GAZPACHO

Le gaspacho de concombre

Freshness with vitamins. To savor, for example, with slices of red pepper bread or unsweetened pound cake (recipes on pages 134 and 136) topped with eggplant caviar. Ideal for a light supper with cold poultry.

●

Chop the onion and garlic. Peel the cucumbers, halve them lengthwise, scrape out the seeds with a small spoon, set aside some cucumber for garnish, thinly slice the rest.

Heat the oil and butter in a pan, add the chopped onion, and cook without browning. Add the garlic and cucumber, stir and cook uncovered for 5 minutes, add the chicken bouillon concentrate, 3 cups (75 cl) of water, thyme flowers, pinch of cayenne pepper, salt, and freshly ground pepper. Cook 10 minutes, then add the cream. Simmer briefly.

Remove from the heat and purée the cooked vegetables with an immersion blender adding some of the mint leaves. Let cool in refrigerator 1 hour or more.

Quickly blanch, peel, seed, and dice the tomato. Using the melon baller, shape small balls from the remaining cucumber. Blanch in salted boiling water and drain.

Pour the gazpacho into the soup tureen. Add the tomato dice and cucumber balls. Cool in refrigerator for 1 hour.

Just before serving, sprinkle the remaining chopped mint leaves on the soup.

Degree of difficulty: **Easy**
Preparation time: **30 minutes**

Kitchen equipment:
Chef's knife or cleaver
Blender
Pot
Immersion blender
Small melon baller

Ingredients:
2 large English cucumbers
1 large onion
1 garlic clove
1 tomato, medium
1 tsp. olive oil
1 tsp. butter
1 tsp. chicken bouillon concentrate
2 sprigs thyme, leaves picked
A pinch cayenne pepper
Salt and pepper
½ cup (12 cl) whipping cream
A pinch celery salt
1 spring mint

Serves 4

MELON SOUP WITH SPICES AND HAM

La soupe de melon aux épices et jambon

●

Serves 4

Peel and seed the melon, cut it into chunks and purée with the lemon juice in a blender. Add the cloves, nutmeg, and water until you obtain the consistency of a soup.

Dice the ham, add to the soup.

Add some fresh ground pepper, place in the refrigerator. To serve, decorate with mint leaves.

A tonic that provides a change of pace for a hot evening. Serve with slices of good country or poppy seed bread and slices of ham.

Degree of difficulty: **Easy**
Preparation time: **10 minutes**

Kitchen equipment:
Blender or immersion blender
Bowl or a large serving dish

Ingredients:
1 large cantaloupe or *Charentais*
** melon**
1 lemon, juice only
3 cloves
A pinch grated nutmeg
Pepper
A few mint leaves
2½ in. slices ham

COLD BEET SOUP AND SMASHED POTATOES

La soupe aux betteraves et ses pommes de terre écrasées

●

Peel and chop the beets. Place them in a pot with 2½ quarts (2,5 l) of boiling water, cook 10 minutes, add salt. Then add the cream and purée through the food mill. The soup becomes translucent and a superb ruby color.

Break and whisk the eggs, and quickly stir them into the hot soup, strain through a fine china cap.

Correct the seasoning and let cool in refrigerator.

Before serving, boil the unpeeled potatoes in salted water. Peel and smash using a fork, add butter or cream, and nutmeg.

Serve at once with the cold soup and hot potatoes.

Alternately eat some hot potatoes and a few spoonfuls of cold soup.

This soup can also be served with red beet chips, prepared by thinly slicing the raw beets and frying them in oil.

An unusual recipe, a reinterpretation of a classic East European soup. Wonderful to savor after a long stroll that has made you both thirsty and hungry. The duo of soup and smashed potatoes results in a balanced and nutritious dish. For the dishes, provide bowls for the soup and plates for the smashed potatoes.

Degree of difficulty: **Easy**
Preparation time: **30 minutes**

Kitchen equipment:
Chef's knife or cleaver
8 qt. pot
Food mill with fine disk
Fine china cap

Ingredients:
1 lb. 2 oz. (500 g) red beets, cooked
3 tbsp. crème fraîche
3 whole eggs
12 potatoes
2 tbsp. butter or ¼ cup cream
A pinch grated nutmeg
Salt and pepper

Serves 6

CHILLED TOMATO SOUP WITH HERBS

La soupe glacée de tomates aux herbes

●

Peel, seed, and cut the tomatoes into chunks. Thinly slice the onions, cut the zucchini into pieces. Cook all the vegetables in the olive oil, add salt, the herbs, and 1½ qts. (1,5 l) of water, cook 20 minutes, and then purée in a blender.

Season with the two ground peppers and fennel seeds.

Let cool in the refrigerator and serve chilled.

A vegetable soup with all the Mediterranean summer flavors. It can be served with cold stuffed tomatoes and mixed greens or arugula tossed with olive oil vinaigrette garnished with thin Parmesan shavings.

Degree of difficulty: **Easy**
Preparation time: **30 minutes**

Kitchen equipment:
6 qt. pot
Blender or immersion blender
Pot

Ingredients:
8 tomatoes, blanched
4 zucchini, peeled
2 onions, peeled
4 tbsp. olive oil
1 tbsp. salt
3 sprigs each mint, basil, and
    tarragon
1½ qts. (1,5 l) water
1 tsp. each black and white pepper,
    ground
½ tsp. fennel seeds

AVOCADO GAZPACHO

Le gaspacho d'avocats

●

Halve the avocados, remove the pits, peel and dice the pulp.

Thinly slice the celery stalks. Peel, seed, and dice the cucumbers. Seed and dice the green pepper.

Peel and very finely chop the garlic cloves and onions.

Transfer the vegetables into the serving bowl, add the tomato juice, season to taste with vinegar, salt, and a few drops of Tabasco.

Let marinate in the refrigerator and serve chilled with lemon wedges.

A delicate tropical touch added to a traditional gazpacho recipe. Serve with grilled bread and guacamole, followed by a large tomato, basil, and mozzarella salad enhanced with olive oil.

Degree of difficulty: **Easy**
Preparation time: **30 minutes**

Kitchen equipment:
Chef's knife or cleaver
2 qt. serving bowl

Ingredients:
2 avocados, ripe to the touch
1 celery stalk
1 cucumber
1 green pepper
4 cloves of garlic
6 small onions
3 cups (75 cl) tomato juice
1 tbsp. red wine vinegar
Salt
Tabasco
4 to 8 lemon wedges

Serves 4

TOMATO GAZPACHO AND BASIL *PALMIERS*

Le gaspacho de tomates et ses palmiers au basilic

A genuine gazpacho, like the ones savored on jasmine fragranced terraces in Spain. It is rich in vitamins as a freshly prepared vegetable juice cocktail, and served with irresistible basil *palmiers* (heart-shaped puff pastry), to satisfy one's appetite.

Degree of difficulty: **Easy for the gazpacho. And if *palmiers* are made with prepared puff pastry dough, no special skill is required.**
Preparation time: **15 minutes for the gazpacho. 1 hour with the preparation of the *palmiers*.**

Kitchen equipment:
Blender
2 qt. serving bowl
Food processor
Baking sheet
Freezer is indispensable for the
    palmiers

Ingredients:
4 large tomatoes, blanched
1 red pepper
1 cucumber
1 garlic clove
1 small onion
¼ cup + 3 tbsp. virgin olive oil
Salt
For approximately 25 palmiers:
9 oz. (250 g) puff pastry dough
4 garlic cloves
1 bunch basil
Olive oil
Coarse sea salt

Peel, halve, seed, and dice the tomatoes. Wash, dry, and seed the pepper, then cut it into small chunks. Peel the cucumber, halve lengthwise to remove the seeds, and thinly slice. Peel the garlic and onion and slice.

Put all these vegetables into the blender, add a ¼ cup of olive oil and some salt. Purée until you obtain a smooth consistency. Pour into a serving bowl and refrigerate.

The *palmiers* may be served warm or at room temperature.

In a food processor, purée the basil and garlic with 3 tbsp. olive oil until you obtain a thick paste. Roll out the puff pastry dough on a lightly floured surface into a ¼ in. (½ cm) thick by 15 × 12 in. (40 × 30 cm) rectangle. Spread the basil paste on the dough, and roll the two wide sides into the center to meet and obtain two twin rolls. Brush them with olive oil. Set aside 30 minutes in the freezer.

Preheat the oven to about 375°F (190°C). Remove the dough roll from the freezer and cut it into ½ in. thick (1 cm) slices. Lightly coat a baking sheet with oil and lay the slices on it; sprinkle with coarse sea salt, and bake about 15 minutes.

Serves 4 to 5

ELEGANT SOUPS

Soups are not meant only for the nice and simple daily life; they may also contain luxurious ingredients and be served elegantly, to become worthy of a king's meal. Here are some sumptuous recipes— three were "swiped" from great chefs (with their generous consent). They will enable you to entertain elegantly, particularly since you will want to serve them with flair in the spirit, the *mise en scène* they deserve.

2

EGG CUSTARD SOUP WITH TRUFFLE

Le lait de poule à la truffe

A culinary masterpiece, reserved for exceptional occasions, which hides its fragrant creaminess under a golden pastry lid. It would be very suitable for a light and elegant small midnight supper on Christmas or New Year's Eve.

Degree of difficulty: **Moderate,** *with great care*
Preparation time: **30 minutes**

Kitchen equipment:
2 qt. heavy bottom pot
1 qt. bowl
Wooden spoon
Ladle
Four small ovenproof ramekins
A pastry brush

Ingredients:
2 cups (50 cl) milk
6 egg yolks
1 canned truffle
1 tbsp. heavy cream
9 oz. (250 g) puff pastry dough
1 whole egg
Salt and pepper

Serves 4

In a pot, heat the milk with ½ tsp. of fine salt. In a bowl, beat a little hot milk with the egg yolks, pour into the pot with the hot milk and thicken, stirring continuously with a wooden spoon, as if making an egg custard. When this mixture coats the spoon, remove from the heat.

Cut four large slices from the truffle and finely chop the remainder.

Fold the heavy cream and chopped truffles into the soup. Ladle equal amounts of the soup into the ramekins. Place a truffle slice and pour one fourth of the juice from the truffle can on each.

Preheat the oven to 425°F (220°C). Thinly roll down the puff pastry dough. Cut 4 circles, slightly larger than the ramekins. Moisten the edges of each ramekin with water, cover with a dough circle overlapping the edges and carefully press to seal it well.

Whisk the whole egg and brush onto the "lids." Draw a lattice with the tip of a knife, being careful not to cut through the dough.

Place the ramekins in the oven and bake 15 minutes, until the dough is puffed and golden.

LAMB'S LETTUCE SOUP WITH SCALLOPS, CORAL FLAN, AND TRUFFLE CAVIAR TOASTS

La soupe de mâches aux saint-jacques, son flan de corail et ses tartines de caviar de truffes

Serves 4

●

Peel and thinly slice the shallots. Carefully wash, spin dry, and coarsely chop the lamb's lettuce. In a pot, brown the shallots in the butter, add the lamb's lettuce, let sweat a little, add one quart (1 l) of water, cook 5 to 6 minutes, purée with a blender, and return to the pot. Add the starch, diluted in a bit of water, and briefly bring to a boil. Keep warm.

For the coral flan, combine all the ingredients for the flan. Pour equal amounts of the mixture into the ramekins. Cover with aluminum foil. Place and cook in a hot water bath for 10 minutes in a preheated 400°F (200°C) oven.

Meanwhile, thinly slice across the raw scallops. Mince the truffle pieces as fine as possible.

Just before serving, add the crème fraîche to the hot soup, ladle into soup plates. Arrange an unmolded coral flan in the center of each plate surrounded by scallop "petals" and optional truffle slices.

Serve with toasted bread slices topped with chopped truffle pieces and a sprinkling of olive oil.

If you announce that you will entertain with a simple lamb's lettuce soup, you will, without doubt, only receive a courteous interest. Don't say anything else and the surprise will only be greater.

Degree of difficulty: Moderate, but no more
Preparation time: 20 minutes

Kitchen equipment:
2 qt. heavy bottom pot
A blender or immersion blender
Four small ovenproof ramekins
Roasting pan for water bath
Aluminum foil

Ingredients:
2 shallots
12 oz. (350 g) lamb's lettuce
1 tbsp. potato starch
1 tbsp. butter
Crème fraîche to taste
One to two scallops per person
16 truffle slices (optional)
For the coral flan:
3½ oz. (100 g) coral (scallop roe)
1 egg
3 tbsp. (5 cl) heavy cream
For the bread slices:
Country bread
1 can truffle pieces
Olive oil for sprinkling

COTRIADE IN PUFF PASTRY CRUST

La cotriade en croûte feuilletée

●

Peel and slice the potatoes crosswise. Thinly slice the leeks, carrots, and onions. Peel and chop the garlic.

In a pot, melt the butter and sweat the vegetables 1 to 2 minutes. Cover with 2 quarts (2 l) of water, season with salt, pepper, bay leaf, thyme, and savory, simmer 15 to 20 minutes.

Divide up the vegetables, fish, and mussels among the four ramekins. Fill with the bouillon.

Cut out four circles from the puff pastry dough slightly larger than the ramekins to fold over the edge. Moisten the edge of each ramekin with bouillon, cover it with a dough circle and press around the edge to seal the lid. Brush with beaten egg. Draw a lattice pattern with the tip of a knife, careful not to cut through the dough. Put into the hot oven at 425°F (220°C) about 15 minutes, until the dough is puffed and golden. Serve immediately from the oven.

Fish and potatoes *cotriade* is to the Brittany coast what bouillabaisse is to the Mediterrannean shore. Simple and succulent, it is elegantly attractive when simmered under an appetizing puff pastry crust in individual ramekins.

Degree of difficulty: Moderate
Preparation time: **1 hour**

Kitchen equipment:
4 qt. pot
Four medium ovenproof ramekins

Ingredients:
1¾ lbs. (800 g) potatoes
2 leeks
2 carrots, peeled
2 onions, peeled
2 garlic cloves
2 tbsp. (30 g) butter
2 qts. (2 l) water
Salt and pepper
Bay leaf, thyme, savory
4 small mackerel fillets
4 chunks monkfish
4 small red mullet fillets
4 small sole fillets
(you may choose other fish; it is imperative, however, to only use fillets)
1 lb. (450 g) mussels, cleaned
1 piece puff pastry dough
1 egg, beaten

CREAM OF LETTUCE SOUP WITH CAVIAR

La crème de laitue au caviar

●

Wash the lettuces and halve them. Immerse them into 2 quarts (2 l) of boiling water for 1 minute. Drain and cool in cold water.

Peel the onion and carrot and finely chop.

Dice the smoked slab bacon.

Melt the butter in a pot and add the onions, carrots, bacon, and 3 shredded lettuces (the fourth is used for decoration). Cover and cook over low heat for 15 minutes without browning. Add the chicken stock, bouquet garni, and crème fraîche. Cook 1 hour over low heat and purée with a blender.

Pour the hot cream of lettuce soup into the plates. Mold spoonfuls of caviar, place them into the remaining lettuce leaves, and float them on the lettuce soup.

The smoothness of lettuce married with the distinctive flavor of caviar is the gastronomic delight to choose for an evening when you really want to treat and surprise. Going by the French proverb, *"Quand on aime on ne compte pas"* ("Love entails generosity"), we provide you with a sumptuous recipe for six persons. But if you divide the quantities by three you will have the finest romantic dinner for two, knowing that caviar is said to be an aphrodisiac.

Degree of difficulty: **Easy**
Preparation time: **1 hour 20 minutes, cooking time included**

Kitchen equipment:
4 qt. pot
Blender or immersion blender

Ingredients:
4 boston lettuces
1 onion
1 carrot
1 bouquet garni
3 oz. (100 g) smoked slab bacon
4 tbsp. (50 g) butter
3⅓ cups (80 cl) rich chicken stock
1 cup (25 cl) crème fraîche
4 oz. (120 g) caviar

Serves 6

PHEASANT CONSOMMÉ WITH CHESTNUTS AND QUENELLES

Le consommé de faisan aux marrons et ses quenelles

●

Serves 6 to 8

Cut and remove the pheasant's breast meat to be used for the quenelles. Lightly brown the pheasant's carcass with the legs and giblets in a very hot oven. Deglaze with white wine.

Prepare the consommé with the beef, pheasant, 3½ quarts (3,5 l) of water and the deglazed pan juices. Using a skimmer, remove any fat on the water surface at the beginning of cooking. Add the garlic, clove studded onion, all the vegetables, thinly sliced, and the bouquet garni. Let simmer for 2 hours. When the meat is cooked, correct seasoning and strain the consommé through cheesecloth.

While the consommé simmers, start working on the chestnuts. Slightly cut the bulging side and roast in the oven, at 450°F (232°C) 8 to 10 minutes, so that their shells burst. Let cool and peel, carefully remove both shell and skin.

Pour 1 cup (25 cl) of the consommé into a pot, add the chestnuts and the star anise. Cover, and simmer 40 minutes. Reserve, keeping warm.

For the quenelles, grind the breast meat using a food grinder with a fine disk. Mix with one beaten egg, salt, and pepper, fold in the crème fraîche and mix thoroughly. Using two teaspoons, shape small quenelles and poach them for a few minutes in salted boiling water.

Evenly divide the chestnuts among the soup plates. Fill with broth. Garnish with the pheasant quenelles and sprinkle with chervil.

The most sumptuous of fall dinners—vegetables, pheasant, and chestnuts that you may have gathered yourself in the forest. As for the pheasant, there are excellent butchers—you may have hunting dinners without hunters.

Degree of difficulty: **Moderate**
Preparation time: **3½ hours,
cooking time included**

**Kitchen equipment:
Roasting pan
6 qt. stockpot
2 qt. pot
Food grinder with a very fine disk
Cheesecloth**

**Ingredients:
1 large pheasant
1 cup white wine
1 lb. (450 g) stewing beef
2 garlic cloves
1 onion studded with a clove
11 oz. (350 g) carrots
11 oz. (350 g) leeks
11 oz. (350 g) celery
11 oz. (350 g) tomatoes
1 bouquet garni
Salt and pepper
1 egg
½ cup (12 cl) crème fraîche
11 oz. (350 g) chestnuts
1 star anise
chervil, snipped**

CHICKEN CONSOMMÉ AND FOIE GRAS PROFITEROLES

Le consommé de volaille et ses profiteroles au foie gras

●

One day ahead, prepare the chicken consommé with the stewing hen, place it in a stock pot with 3 quarts (3 l) of water, slice and add all the vegetables, salt, and pepper. Let simmer 2 hours, skim regularly to remove fat, and let the liquid reduce by half. Cool in the refrigerator.

Once the consommé is cold, skim off any fat floating on the surface, remove the meat and vegetables, strain the consommé through a fine china cap, and clarify it by slowly heating it up with one beaten egg white which, by coagulating, precipitates and carries away all impurities. Let rest and strain again.

To make the profiteroles, put the water into a pot, add the butter cut in small chunks and 2 tsp. salt. Bring to a boil and reduce the heat. When the butter is melted, remove from the heat; add the paprika and flour, stir continuously with a wooden spoon.

Return the pot to the heat, cook and stir until the mixture forms a ball and comes away from the sides of the pot.

Off the heat, add one egg and thoroughly beat it into the mixture; break the second egg in a bowl and beat with a fork, fold half of the egg into the dough, mix well.

Lightly butter a baking sheet. Using a pastry bag or a spoon, pipe ¾ in. (2 cm) mounds onto it. Brush them with the remainder of beaten egg. Bake in a preheated 400°F (200°C) oven for about 10 minutes. Turn the oven

Again a balanced dish, to be prepared one day ahead, based on chicken consommé, followed by a salad, which will be the delicate part of Christmas Eve or New Year's Eve midnight supper or a fine dinner. Despite its sumptuous appearance, it is relatively easy to prepare successfully and requires only time and care.

Degree of difficulty: **Moderate. Easy if you buy ready-made profiteroles (mini puff buns).**
Preparation time: **Approximately 4 hours, cooking time included**

Kitchen Equipment:
6 qt. stock pot
Fine china cap
2 qt. pot
Pastry bag
Fine-meshed drum sieve
Baking sheet
Wooden spoon

Ingredients:
1 stewing hen
1 each: carrot, white turnip, onion, leek, celery stalk
Coarse salt and peppercorns
1 egg white
For the profiteroles:
⅓ cup (8 cl) water
2 tbsp. (30 g) butter
1½ tsp. paprika
⅓ cup (50 g) flour
2 eggs
5 oz. (150 g) foie gras
A dash of port
Salt and pepper
1 red pepper
1 bunch chervil

off. Partially open the oven door and leave the profiteroles 5 more minutes before removing them to a wire rack to cool.

Prepare the foie gras filling. With a spoon meticulously smash it through a fine drum sieve until it is very smooth. Add the dash of port. (The foie gras may also be puréed with this port using a food processor.)

Using a pastry bag, fill the profiteroles with foie gras.

To serve, bring the consommé you prepared the day before to a boil. Lay three or four profiteroles in each soup plate, decorate with diced red pepper and chervil. Ladle the hot consommé at the last moment and offer the remaining profiteroles on a plate, or else serve the consommé in a soup tureen and the profiteroles on the side.

●

Accelerated version:

In case you are in a hurry, you may use a good store bought chicken broth and small prepared profiteroles to be filled. The only thing to prepare will be the foie gras mousse—the result will not leave you blushing.

GREAT CHEFS AND THEIR SEAFOOD SOUPS

Les chefs et leurs soupes aux fruits de mer

●

OYSTERS IN TOMATO BOUILLON
Les huîtres en bouillon de tomates

by Olivier Roellinger, the master chef of Maisons de Bricourt in Cancale, France, a two star in the Michelin red guide.

Base preparation: 1 to 2 hours in advance, lightly toast all spices, except the *niora*. Grind in a coffee grinder and sift if necessary. Keep in an airtight container.

Wash and dry the small bunches of wild purslane. Pick the thyme and lemon basil leaves.

Prepare the bouillon: Cut the two pieces of lemon peel into fine julienne and blanch twice. Put them to candy for 1 hour with a little water and the brown sugar, then drain, chop very finely, and reserve.

Drizzle the garlic with oil and roast in the oven. Finely slice the onions. Remove the stems from the tomatoes, cut a cross into them and immerse into boiling water for 10 seconds. Then shock them with cold water; this way the skin comes off easily. Cut them up widthwise, seed them with a small spoon into a fine-mesh strainer reserving the juice. Peel the galangal, and mince.

Slowly brown the onion with the galangal, in butter. Add the sugar and 2 tablespoons of the spice mixture. Cook 10 seconds, add the vinegar, and briefly bring to a boil. Add the garlic, lemon peel, mango, tomatoes, basil, salt, and the reserved tomato juice. Bring just to a boil and simmer over low heat for 1¼ hours.

To end the elegant soup festival with fireworks, here are three recipes from great chefs who are inspired by seafood. Exquisite and spectacular, these recipes do not require any professional skills to be successful. Creativity with these recipes is far more important than technical skills.

OYSTERS IN TOMATO BOUILLON

Degree of difficulty: **Easy**
Preparation time: **Fast final stage**

Ingredients:
2 oz. (50 g) wild purslane
Lemon basil leaves
Thyme sprig
2 pieces lemon peel
1 tbsp. brown sugar
10 large ripe tomatoes
2 onions
½ mango
A 3 oz. (80 g) galangal piece (or ginger root)
1 tbsp. sugar
2 tbsp. rice vinegar
3 garlic cloves
2 large basil sprigs
4 tbsp. (50 g) butter
Fine salt
2 dozen Pacific Oysters, large
2 dozen Olympia Oysters, large
Spice mixture:
1 tbsp. cardamom
2 star anise
2 cloves
3 tbsp. mace
1 tbsp. *niora* (mild chili)
10 tbsp. coriander seeds

Serves 4

Remove the garlic and basil. Pour into a fine-mesh strainer and let drain slowly, do not press it through, and save the bouillon. In this way a jam is obtained in the strainer and the clear bouillon flows into the pot.

Open the oysters, loosen them, and keep them in their juice. Check and clean any shell particles.

Last minute: Reheat the tomato bouillon without boiling it. Slowly reheat the jam. Slowly bring the oysters in their juice to a temperature of 150°F (65°C).

Into each soup plate, lay a jam *quenelle* with 6 warm oysters, sprinkle with thyme and lemon peel. Pour the bouillon over the oysters, finish with a small bunch of purslane.

This soup may also be served cold.

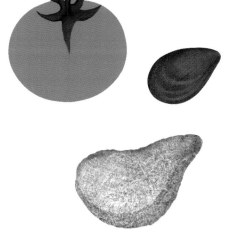

Serves 4

OYSTER MINESTRONE WITH PESTO
Le minestrone d'huîtres au pistou
by Jean-Paul Hartmann, *L'Almandin* restaurant, île de la Lagune in Saint Cyprien, France, a one star in the Michelin red guide.

Peel the carrots and turnips, shell the garden peas and fava beans, and snap the ends off the string beans. Cut all vegetables into small ¼ in. (5 mm) dice.

Open and shuck the oysters, keeping them in their juice. Blanch the basil in a little boiling water and purée it in a food processor with 6 tbsp. of olive oil, the chopped garlic, salt, and pepper, to make a pesto.

Sweat all vegetables in a pan with the remaining olive oil, season with salt and pepper, add the chicken bouillon. Boil for 2 minutes, remove from the heat, add the oysters and pesto. To serve, place the vegetables in the bottom of each soup plate, arrange six oysters over them and generously cover with the chicken bouillon.

OYSTER MINESTRONE
WITH PESTO

Degree of difficulty: **Easy**
Preparation time: **About 45 minutes**

Kitchen equipment:
Pot
Stewpot
Food Processor

Ingredients:
2 oz. (60 g) carrots
2 oz. (60 g) white turnips
2 oz. (60 g) garden peas
2 oz. (60 g) fava beans
2 oz. (60 g) string beans
1 bunch fresh basil
10 tbsp. olive oil
1 tsp. chopped garlic
Salt and pepper
24 oysters
2½ cups (6 dl) chicken bouillon

MUSSEL AND CLAM SOUP WITH SAFFRON
La soupe de moules et palourdines au safran
by Jean-Paul Hartmann, *L'Almondin* restaurant, île de la Lagune in Saint Cyprien, France, a one star in the Michelin red guide.

Evenly distribute the shallots and white wine between two pots. Drop the washed and scraped mussels into one of them, the clams into the other. Cover and cook until they open completely, shell them, reserve, and strain their juices through a fine china cap. Combine the two cooking liquids together into one pot, slightly reduce the liquid, add the crème fraîche, saffron, and further reduce until a light cream is obtained. Keep warm.

Sauté the julienne vegetables with olive oil in a frying pan, until they are cooked but still firm.

Add the vegetables and the shucked shellfish to the soup, briefly bring to a boil, and serve in a soup tureen.

●

CHILLED LANGOUSTINE CONSOMMÉ
Le consommé glacé de langoustines
by Christian Tetedoie, chef from Lyon, France, elected best craftsperson of France, 1996, a one star in Michelin red guide.

Shell the langoustine tails and keep cold. Crush the legs in a mortar, sauté in some olive oil with one each chopped carrot and onion, and the tomato concentrate. Once the mixture is browned, deglaze with the white wine and cognac, add 2 quarts (2 l) of water, the bouquet garni, salt, and one tomato. Cook slowly for 1 hour.

Whisk the egg whites, pour them together with the remaining tomato into the hot bouillon to clarify it, strain, let cool in the refrigerator. Peel the ginger root with a paring knife, cut it into small dice, add the sugar, barely cover with water and cook 30 minutes. Cut the remaining carrot, onion, and turnip, into a very small dice and braise in olive oil.

Put the langoustine tails on the baking sheet, sprinkle with fine sea salt and roast for 3 minutes in a hot oven.

MUSSEL AND CLAM SOUP
WITH SAFFRON

Degree of difficulty: **Easy**
Preparation time: **30–40 min.**

Kitchen equipment:
Two pots
Frying pan
Fine china cap

Ingredients:
4 small shallots, peeled and sliced
2 lbs. (1 kg) mussels
2 lbs. (1 kg) clams
1¼ cup (3 dl) white wine
2 cups (50 cl) crème fraîche
Saffron powder or stigmas
4 oz. (100 g) each carrots, leeks,
    and celery root cut into julienne
2 tbsp. olive oil

CHILLED LANGOUSTINE
CONSOMMÉ

Degree of difficulty: **Moderate**
Preparation time: **About 1¾ hours**

Kitchen equipment:
Mortar and pestle
3 qt. pot
Small pot
Paring knife
Baking sheet
Frying pan

Ingredients:
2 lbs. (1 kg) langoustines
2 carrots
2 onions
1 tbsp. tomato concentrate
1 cup (¼ l) white wine
½ cup (1 dl) cognac
2 tomatoes, cut into quarters
1 white turnip
1 bouquet garni
2 egg whites
1 fresh ginger root
¼ cup (50 g) sugar
½ cup (1 dl) olive oil
Salt
8 sprigs chervil

Arrange the diced vegetables, thoroughly drained, in the soup plates, add a little ginger to taste, fill with the thoroughly chilled consommé and, at the last moment, add the hot scampi and some chopped chervil.

●

And finally a last minute stylish soup:

FISH SOUP AND OYSTER KEBAB
Soupe de poisson et brochette d'huîtres
Shuck the oysters, reserve their liquid, and slowly poach them for 1 minute in their juice. Drain, dry with paper towels, and dredge in the flour, then whisked egg, and breadcrumbs.

Skewer them, alternating with the bacon chunks, and pan fry in hot oil.

Meanwhile, strain the oyster liquid, add to the fish soup, reheat thoroughly, and serve the soup in a soup tureen and the kebabs on the side.

●

Other variation:

OYSTER *PARMENTIÈRE* AND CRISP BACON
La parmentière d'huîtres au lard croustillant
Plan for, or have a classic potato leek soup, puréed with a food mill or blender, ready. Add some crème fraîche.

Shuck the oysters and poach them for 1 minute in their juice. Drain. Using the oil, brown the sliced bacon in a frying pan, until very crisp.

Heat the soup and put into soup plates, place the oysters and sliced bacon on top.

FISH SOUP AND OYSTER KEBAB

Degree of difficulty: Easy
Preparation time: Depending on the number of persons, and the oysters you need to open.

Kitchen equipment:
1 qt. pot
Frying pan
One skewer per person

Ingredients:
Per person
6 oysters
6 chunks slab bacon
Flour
1 egg, whisked
Very fine breadcrumbs
¾ cup canned or frozen fish soup

OYSTER *PARMENTIÈRE* AND CRISP BACON

Degree of difficulty: Easy
Preparation time: Depending on the number of persons, and the oysters you need to open.

Kitchen equipment:
Pot
Frying pan

Ingredients:
Per person
¾ cup potato leek soup
1 tbsp. crème fraîche
4 to 6 large oysters
4 to 6 thin slices smoked bacon
½ tbsp. oil

EUPHORIANT SOUPS

It can be easily understood from the title that they stem from the peasant *chabrot* tradition, that is, an addition of red wine. Whether they are enriched by beer, white wine, or a marc brandy, all these soups are alcoholic. Even if the cooking neutralizes the alcohol content, they are reserved for "grown-ups." They are all nutritious, generate heat in the body, and are highly recommended winter dishes, especially since most come in duo with hearty accompaniments.

BEER SOUP AND WAFFLES

La soupe à la bière et ses gaufres

●

Ahead of time, prepare the waffle batter: melt the butter over low heat, let cool, add the 2 whole eggs, yolk, nutmeg, and salt.

Fold in the flour by sprinkling it, and dilute with water to obtain a smooth and liquid batter. If lumps form, pour the batter through a medium china cap to remove them. Reserve.

Shortly before serving, cook the waffles and keep them warm.

20 minutes before serving, rub the sugar cubes on the lemon peel until they become yellow. Pour the beer into a 2 qt. pot together with the sugar, cloves, and cinnamon. Bring to a boil. Dilute the cornstarch in the cold water. Pour into the beer, stirring well and cook 3 minutes.

Separate the whites from the egg yolks. Whisk the egg yolks until frothy, then whisk them into the soup.

Add salt and pepper, then slowly pour in the crème fraîche to obtain a very creamy mixture. Keep warm.

At the last moment, beat the egg whites to stiff peaks.

Bring salted water to a simmer.

Using a spoon, shape small egg white "meringue" balls and carefully place them into the simmering water; cook until they are firm.

Pour the soup into a soup tureen or large bowls, and serve it with the "meringues."

It makes a real meal for very hearty appetites, with rich Flemish flavors and the successful as much as unusual combination of beer and spices. A choice winter soup.

Degree of difficulty: **Moderate**
Preparation time: **1 hour**

Kitchen equipment:
2 qt. pot
Large pot
Mixing bowl
Mixer
Waffle iron

Ingredients:
4 sugar cubes
1 lemon
1 quart (1 l) lager beer
2 cloves
1 cinnamon stick
4 tsp. cornstarch
6 tsp. cold water
4 eggs
Salt and pepper
1 cup (2 dl) crème fraîche
For the waffle batter:
1 scant cup (125 g) flour
2 tbsp. (30 g) butter
3⅓ cups (80 cl) water
2 whole eggs
1 egg yolk
1 tsp. (5 g) nutmeg
1 tsp. (5 g) salt

If preferred, the "meringue" may be substituted with eggs poached in beer.

Pour the beer into the pot and bring to a boil. One by one break each egg into a cup, and carefully slide them into the boiling beer, simmer about 3 minutes, remove with a skimmer and quickly immerse in a bowl filled with iced water to stop the cooking.

Serve the soup and waffles together.

SAUTERNES BOUILLON AND TIED BEEF

Le bouillon au sauternes et son boeuf à la ficelle

●

To begin with, for the first bouillon combine the stew beef, the bones, 5 quarts (5 l) of water, salt, cloves, and the bouquet garni. Cook for 2 hours; in the meantime clean the leeks, fennel, and celery, and peel the turnips, onions, and carrots.

Keeping the stew beef for another use, strain the bouillon through a fine china cap, return to the stockpot and drop in all vegetables, celery and leeks tied into a bundle. Cook for three fourths of the total cooking time (about 30 minutes), add the second piece of meat, tightly tied beforehand, cook for 20 minutes, then reduce the heat to low and let simmer for 20 more minutes.

Transfer enough bouillon to fill a large pot and poach the marrowbones in it for 5 minutes.

Meat, vegetables, and bouillon—it's the sumptuous version of a family stew, made to warm and fully satisfy a table of hungry gourmands. It requires a little more preparation time than most of our other recipes, but it's worth it.

Degree of difficulty: **Easy. Just a little patience and care is required.**
Preparation time: **3½ to 4 hours**

Kitchen equipment:
Large stockpot
Two large pots
Fine china cap
Butcher's twine

Ingredients:
For the first bouillon:
1 lb. (500 g) stew beef
2 beef bones
5 quarts (5 l) water
Salt
2 Cloves
1 bouquet garni
2 carrots
1 white turnip
2 onions
2 celery stalks
3 leeks
6 marrowbones, cut in 1½ in.
   (3 cm) pieces
For the final bouillon:
3 lbs. (1,5 kg) beef
   fillet, thin-sliced beef
6 carrots
4 white turnips
6 leeks
1 celery stalk
3 fennels
1 pinch curry powder
4 glasses Sauternes wine

Keep the meat and vegetables warm.

Strain the bouillon. Add a pinch of curry powder and Sauternes wine. Bring to a boil and serve at once with the sliced meat, surrounded by the vegetables and marrowbones, accompanied by the hot bouillon and toasted country bread.

With the stew meat of the first bouillon, you can prepare a cottage pie, stuffed tomatoes or cabbage; or simply dice and serve it with a salad sauced with well seasoned shallot vinaigrette.

Other possibility: Prepare a *fleisch schnecke* (see below) to enrich the above dish or replace the tied beef.

●

A variation: FLEISCH SCHNECKE
Une variante: la fleisch schnecke
Prepare the noodle dough by kneading the flour and eggs until the mixture is homogeneous. Wrap it in plastic and refrigerate for 2 hours.

Using a food processor, purée the meat and some vegetables together with the parsley and onion. Season with salt and pepper.

Roll out the dough to a rectangle about ⅛ in. (2 mm) thick. Spread the meat and vegetable filling onto it, leaving an edge of ¾ in. (2 cm) clear.

Roll up into a cylinder, tightly wrap in a clean towel and tie the ends with string.

Bring the bouillon to a simmer, poach the roll in it for 30 minutes, drain, and let cool with the roll lying flat.

Before serving, remove the towel, cut the roll into slices 1 in. (2,5 cm) thick, brown lightly in hot butter over medium heat, about 1 minute on each side, and serve warm or cold on the side of the bouillon, flavored or not with a little Sauternes or red wine.

FLEISCH SCHNECKE

To make a thriftier, more nutritious dish than the tied beef, try this Alsatian specialty that combines meat and noodles with vegetables.

Degree of difficulty: **Easy, despite appearances.**
Preparation time: **2½ hours plus the normal cooking time for a stew, if it is not ready.**

Kitchen equipment:
Stockpot
Food processor
Pastry board and rolling pin
Frying pan
Butcher's twine
A clean towel
Plastic wrap

Ingredients:
In addition to the regular groceries for the stew:
1¼ lbs. (600 g) cooked stew (meat and vegetables)
3 quarts (1,5 l) bouillon
1 onion
1 bunch parsley
Salt and pepper
For the dough:
2 cups (300 g) flour
3 eggs

MUSSEL SOUP WITH ORANGE AND WHITE WINE

La soupe de moules à l'orange et au vin blanc

Peel and chop the shallots. Cut the leek into thin julienne strips.

Put the shallots, leek, wine, and fish stock into the stockpot. Bring to a boil, drop in the mussels, cover and cook until they are all open.

Shell the mussels. Strain the cooking juices through a fine china cap into the 2 qt. pot, place on heat and reduce by one third. At this point, add the crème fraîche, saffron, and reduce by another third.

Grate the orange peel and juice the orange.

Cut the butter into small pieces and whisk into the soup. Finally, add the orange peel and half of the juice. Return the mussels to the pot, long enough to heat them up, and serve in thoroughly heated soup plates.

Serves 6 to 8

Bright colors and delicate flavors; it's a beautiful rich exotic soup, made to delight lovers of mussels and spices. With large country bread slices, it is self-sufficient. A salad, a cheese platter, and the meal is ready.

Degree of difficulty: **Moderate**
Preparation time: **30 minutes**

Kitchen equipment:
stockpot
2 qt. pot
whisk
fine china cap

Ingredients:
3 quarts (3 l) mussels, washed and scrubbed
2 shallots
1 leek, white part
¼ cup (6 cl) white wine
½ cup (10 cl) fish stock (ready-made)
⅔ cup (15 cl) crème fraîche
11 tbsp. (150 g) butter
1 pinch saffron
1 orange
Salt and pepper

FATHER SAINT-RUPH'S TAMIÉ CHEESE AND SAVOY MARC BRANDY SOUP

La soupe au tamié et marc de savoie du père Saint-Ruph

Serves 6 to 8

●

Peel and thinly slice the onions. Stew them in the melted butter, over low heat, covered, until golden brown. Add the brandy and chicken stock and slowly simmer over low heat until reduced by half.

Meanwhile, place the bacon slices in a cold frying pan, cook over low heat until they are brown and crisp. Place on paper towels to remove excess fat, and then chop them.

Coarsely shred the cheese. Combine it with the bacon. Set aside.

Purée the soup with a blender.

Separate the egg whites from the yolks. Thicken the soup with the beaten yolks and the crème fraîche combined. Heat it without boiling it and evenly distribute among the soup bowls.

Beat the egg whites to stiff peaks. Fold in the cheese bacon mixture. Using two spoons, shape large quenelles and place one in each bowl. Place into the oven at 350°F (180°C) about 5 minutes, then finish under a broiler until each meringue inflates and is golden brown. It will then be poached by the soup from beneath and broiled on the top.

Serve at once with thickly sliced warm toast.

Highland, hearty, and pious. Saint Ruph was a hermit monk. He founded the abbey named after him. As for Tamié cheese, the monks of the abbey of the same name make it. Bernard Gay, from the *Gay Séjour* hotel in Faverges, Haute-Savoie (France) gave us this recipe, really made for skiers' appetites. Eat it with warm toasted bread.

Degree of difficulty: **Moderate**
Preparation time: **1 hour**

Kitchen equipment:
Stewpot
Frying pan
Chef's knife or cleaver
Blender or immersion blender
Mixer
As many ovenproof soup bowls or individual soup tureens as there are persons.

Ingredients:
8 onions
7 tbsp. (100 g) butter
1 small glass Savoy marc brandy
1½ quarts (1,5 l) rich chicken stock
4 oz. (100 g) slab smoked bacon, thin slices
6½ to 7 oz. (180 to 200 g) Tamié cheese (or Reblochon)
2 eggs
2 tbsp. crème fraîche
Country style bread

RED WINE SEAFOOD SOUP

La soupe marine en chabrot

●

Open the oysters and reserve their juice after straining it through a fine china cap.

Using two covered pots, separately cook the mussels and cockles. Strain their cooking juices and add them to the oyster juice.

Shuck all shellfish and keep warm.

Cut the leek into thin julienne strips.

Bring the oyster and shellfish juices to a boil. Add a cup of red wine, reduce by ⅓ and then whisk in the butter, cut into small chunks. Remove from the heat and give the pot a circular motion until the butter is totally absorbed by the soup.

Add pepper, and correct seasoning.

Warm up the soup plates. Divide the remaining red wine among them. Arrange the oysters, mussels, and cockles in the plates. Pour over the hot bouillon and sprinkle with the leek julienne.

Here is the seaside soup in which oysters, mussels, and cockles successfully meet with just the right quantity of red wine to give it an even stronger personality. The large slices of country bread spread with sea salt butter and served with the soup match it perfectly.

Degree of difficulty: **Easy**
Preparation time: **45 minutes**

Kitchen equipment:
Several pots
Fine china cap

Ingredients:
12 oysters
24 mussels
24 cockles
1 leek, white part
1½ cups red wine
7 tbsp. (100 g) butter
Pepper

BEAUFORT CHEESE SOUP AND CROUTONS

La soupe de fromage au beaufort et ses croûtons

●

In a heavy bottomed pot, melt the butter, sprinkle with the flour, stir with a wooden spoon, add the white wine and bouillon. Add the garlic, pepper, grated nutmeg, and a little salt.

Bring to a boil while still stirring, and slowly add the shredded cheese. As soon as it is melted, remove the pot from the heat.

Whisk the yolks with the crème fraîche and pour into a soup tureen, ladle the very hot soup over it, sprinkle with chopped parsley, add the diced Beaufort cheese, and serve hot with garlic rubbed croutons, lightly browned in butter.

For hearty appetites, ham slices with a salad may be served.

For cheese amateurs and mountain lovers, here is a soup prepared in the Savoy, France style of fondue, but more original. A crackling wood fire would match its flavor very well.

Degree of difficulty: **Average**
Preparation time: **30 to 45 minutes**

Kitchen equipment:
Large heavy bottomed pot
Soup tureen
Frying pan
Wooden spoon

Ingredients:
4 tbsp. (50 g) butter
⅓ cup (50 g) flour
2 cups (50 cl) dry white wine
1½ quarts (1,5 l) vegetable
    bouillon (made with bouillon
    cubes)
1 garlic clove, chopped
pepper, nutmeg, and salt
5 oz. (150 g) Beaufort cheese,
    shredded
2 egg yolks
4 tbsp. (50 g) crème fraîche
2 oz. (50 g) Beaufort cheese, small
    dice
1 tbsp. chopped parsley

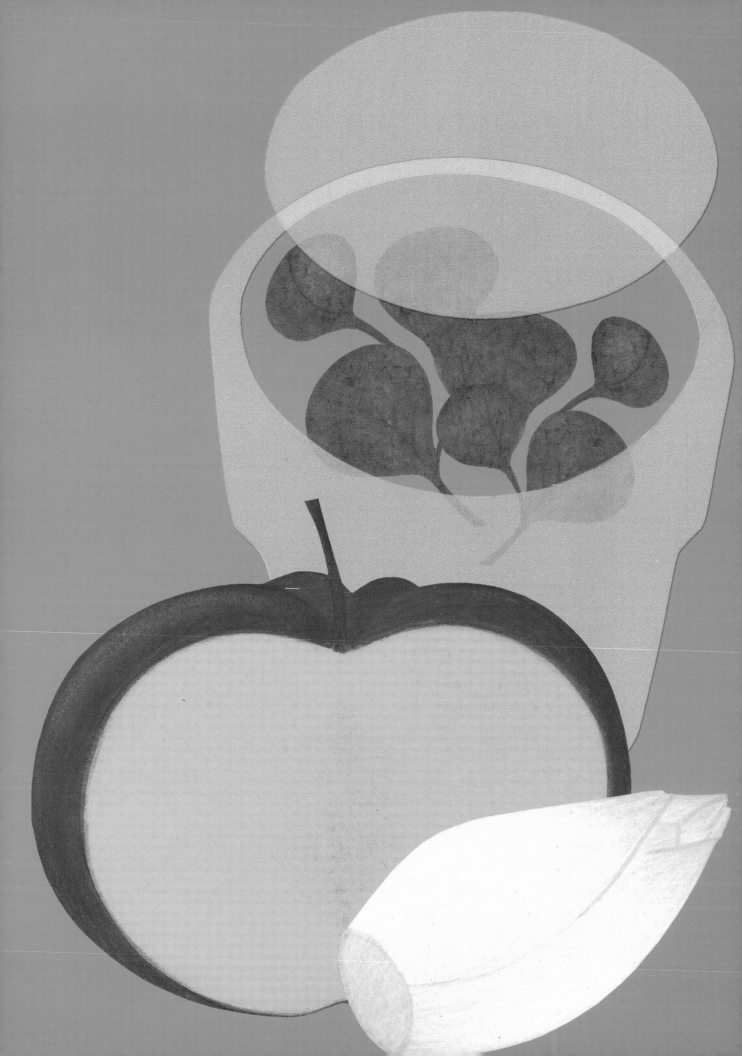

VEGETABLE SOUPS

Our grandmothers would pick a few seasonal vegetables from the garden, take a small stroll in the countryside to pick dandelions, or nettles, and then concoct the most genuine of vegetable soups with their modest find. These soups, as simple and easy, are their direct descendants. It is a way to delight your family with an excellent meal in no time, and at minimal cost. Invariably healthy, you may get the feeling, rational or not, that these vegetable soups awaken in us the memory of ancestral foods.

4

OLD STYLE POT HERB PANADA

La panade aux herbes potagères à l'ancienne

Serves 6

●

Clean, wash, and thinly shred all vegetables. Melt the butter and slowly cook them in it. Reserve.

Dice the bread. Put it into a large pot with 2 qts. (2 l) of water. Cook for just under an hour over low heat, to make a panada.

Then, process the vegetables and bread in a food processor. Add the crème fraîche, salt, and pepper and cook for another 10 minutes over low heat.

Whisk the egg yolk with the lemon juice. Just before serving, whisk it into the panada. Decorate the panada with chopped chives and chervil.

A stylish, tasty and nutritious panada variation, prepared with garden vegetables, the way our grandmothers used to—not wasting a crumb of bread, even if a day old. Followed by a large salad and cheese platter, it makes a solid and complete meal.

Degree of difficulty: **Easy**
Preparation time: **1½ hours**

Kitchen equipment:
Chef's knife or cleaver
1 qt. pot
4 qt. pot
Food processor

Ingredients:
3 tbsp. (40 g) butter
2 leeks
4 leaves green swiss chard, large
7 oz. (200 g) sorrel
9 oz. (250 g) stale bread
1 cup (25 cl) crème fraîche
Salt and pepper
1 egg yolk
½ lemon, juice only
1 handful chives
1 handful chervil

NETTLE SOUP AND SNAIL FRITTERS

La soupe à l'oseille du cantonnier et ses beignets d'escargot

●

Peel and chop the onions. Braise the onions in melted butter, add the nettles, water, salt, and pepper; bring to a boil and simmer 7 minutes. Purée the mixture in a blender. Reserve until serving.

To prepare the fritters, place the flour and breadcrumbs on separate plates, and the eggs in a shallow bowl. Thoroughly drain and dry the snails. Dredge them in the garlic and finely chopped parsley, next in the flour, then the eggs, and finally the breadcrumbs; repeat this twice. Fry by placing them in hot oil one by one, cook until golden. Drain on paper towels, keep warm until ready to serve.

While the fritters are frying, mix the crème fraîche with the cornstarch, whisk into the soup, bring to a brief boil and serve hot in soup plates or a tureen accompanied by the crispy hot snail fritters.

A soup to be prepared in the early spring, when nettles are picked as young and tender shoots. It is a "primitive" soup, like ones that were concocted when people lived off picking and gathering. Ideally, serve this soup in plates with the fritters, also called *cromesquis*, arranged around the soup plate on large assorted or matching dinner plates.

Degree of difficulty: **Easy**
Preparation time: **30 minutes**

Kitchen equipment:
Gloves to pick the nettles
3 qt. stewpot
Chef's knife or cleaver
Blender or immersion blender
Large frying pan

Ingredients:
2 onions
2 tbsp. (25 g) butter
14 oz. (400 g) cleaned nettle
  shoots
1 quart (1 l) water
Salt and pepper
¼ cup (6 cl) crème fraîche or cream
2 tbsp. cornstarch
For the snail fritters:
Provide 6, 9, or 12 snails
  per person, depending on
  appetites (preferably large
  ***Bourgogne* snails)**
1 cup (150 g) flour
3 eggs, beaten
2 cups (300 g) fine breadcrumbs
1 head garlic, finely chopped
1 large bunch parsley
Oil for frying

DANDELION SOUP AND SCRAMBLED EGG SANDWICHES WITH DANDELION FLOWERS

*La soupe de pissenlits et ses tartines
de brouillade aux boutons de pissenlits*

Here we have again a mix of the wild and refined, to be prepared with young dandelions when their flowers are still in bud. It's the ideal dish when spring is still brisk enough for one to need a hot soup, and satisfying enough for one who craves greens. For bread, choose a good country bread, or bake it yourself using one of the recipes from pages 132 to 137.

Degree of difficulty: **Average**
Preparation time: **1½ hours**

Serves 6

●

Wash the dandelions several times in vinegar water, blanch for a few minutes in boiling water, drain, and chop.

Pour a little oil into a 5 qt. pot and lightly brown the two cloves of garlic, add the dandelions and chicken stock, cook 1 hour. This soup may be prepared ahead of time and kept refrigerated until mealtime.

Before serving, whisk the egg yolks into the hot (not boiling) soup, stir briskly, and correct seasoning.

For the scrambled eggs, blanch the dandelion buds about 1 minute in salted water. Drain. Melt the butter in the frying pan, sweat the thinly sliced onion, add the dandelion buds, stir, take off the heat, and reserve.

Lightly whisk the eggs, put them in the nonstick frying pan over low heat, beat continuously with the whisk. When the eggs are a creamy consistency, immediately remove from the heat. Add salt and pepper. Fold in the dandelion buds.

Spread onto the toasted bread slices and serve on the side of the soup.

Kitchen equipment:
Chef's knife or cleaver
Colander
5 qt. pot
Medium frying pan
Wire whisk
Nonstick frying pan

Ingredients:
3 dozen dandelion clusters
2 tbsp. oil
2 garlic cloves
3 quarts (3 l) rich chicken stock
6 egg yolks
Salt and pepper
For the scrambled egg sandwich:
6 large slices of bread
11 oz. (300 g) dandelion
    flower buds
1 onion
8 eggs
1 tbsp. butter
Salt and pepper

PUMPKIN SOUP AU GRATIN AND CROQUETTES

La gratinée de potiron et ses croquettes

Serves 6 to 8

●

Cut the pumpkin top. Scoop out the flesh. Remove seeds and strings. Chunk the flesh.

Clean, wash, and thinly slice the leeks, onion, and garlic.

In the pot melt the butter, add and sweat the leeks, onion, and garlic. Add the pumpkin, milk, stock, a little grated nutmeg, salt, and pepper. Simmer 30 minutes.

Purée in blender and fold in the crème fraîche. Transfer to the ovenproof container or hollow pumpkin. Stew with toasted croutons and sprinkle with grated cheese until covered. Place into the 400°F (200°C) oven (wrapping the pumpkin with parchment paper, if you use it as a soup tureen). Brown it about 15 minutes or less.

Meanwhile, cut the Beaufort cheese into sticks about ¾ by 2⅓ in. (2 cm × 6 cm). Place the flour and breadcrumbs on separate plates, and the eggs whisked together with the oil into a shallow bowl. Coat the sticks with the flour, eggs, and breadcrumbs, fry in 325°F (160°C) oil, drain on paper towels and keep warm.

Either serve in the pumpkin tureen with the croquettes on a plate, or in individual soup tureens on a plate with the croquettes around.

Here's a golden soup that makes you crave autumn. It will make a lasting impression—the addition of the cheese croquettes is sure to satisfy the heartiest of appetites. Individual soup tureens, as pictured, may be used, or the hollow pumpkin may also serve as a soup tureen.

Degree of difficulty: **Easy**
Preparation time: **45 minutes**

Kitchen equipment:
5 qt. pot
Blender or immersion blend
An ovenproof container (if this gratin soup is not to be served in the hollow pumpkin)
Parchment paper (optional if the pumpkin is the tureen)
Fryer

Ingredients:
1 pumpkin, 6½ to 8½ lbs. (3 to 4 kg)
2 tbsp. butter
2 leeks, white part
1 onion
2 garlic cloves
2 cups (½ l) milk
2 cups (½ l) rich chicken stock
A little grated nutmeg
Salt and pepper
¾ cup (20 cl) crème fraîche
Some croutons
Grated cheese
For the croquettes:
11 oz. (300 g) Beaufort cheese
⅓ cup (50 g) flour
2 eggs, beaten
1½ tbsp. (2 cl) peanut oil
1 cup (200 g) fine breadcrumbs

ERMINY POTAGE
ITH MUSSELS

La potage germiny aux moules

Serves 4

Scrape and thoroughly wash the mussels. Peel and chop the shallot. Put them into the pot with white wine, parsley stems, salt, pepper, and mussels. Cook covered for 5 minutes.

Melt the butter in the sauté pan. Add the thoroughly washed sorrel, cook it for 5 minutes, and purée it.

Shell and reserve the mussels; keep the cooking juices. Strain through a fine china cap and add enough water to make 1 quart (1 l) of liquid. Place in the 3 qt., pot with the sorrel purée and the stock. Boil 3 minutes.

Whisk the egg yolks with the crème fraîche and add to the *potage*, which should not boil, stir with a whisk.

Add the shelled mussels, chervil, and serve hot.

Germiny potage is the elegant name for sorrel soup. A great standard of soup gastronomy, renewed here by a mussel duo that makes it a very subtle, balanced and original dish.

Degree of difficulty: **Easy**
Preparation time: **30 minutes**

Kitchen equipment:
Stockpot
Sauté pan
Food processor
Fine china cap
3 qt. pot
Mixing bowl
Wire whisk

Ingredients:
1¾ lbs. (800 g) mussels
1 large (30 g) shallot, chopped
1¼ cups (3 dl) white wine
3 parsley stems
Salt and pepper
1½ tbsp. (20 g) butter
4½ oz. (125 g) sorrel, washed
1 cup (¼ l) chicken stock (can be made from a cube)
4 egg yolks
½ cup (1 dl) crème fraîche
A little chervil

MILK, ENDIVE, AND SCALLION SOUP

La soupe au lait, endives et ciboules

●

Remove the core end from the endives, clean, wash, and thinly slice them crosswise. Peel and cut the potato into a small dice.

Braise the endives in half the butter, add the potato, boiling milk, salt, pepper, and a generous pinch of nutmeg. Cover and simmer for 25 minutes, then purée with a blender. Reserve.

Peel the scallions, keeping the green tops. Cut into large pieces and braise in the remaining butter in the sauté pan about 10 minutes, without browning.

Return the soup to the heat, add the scallions, cook for 5 more minutes.

Serve with golden toasted croutons.

A winter soup that enhances the full flavor of endives, without bitterness. It can be an entreé when served with toasted croutons—and preceded by a terrine and salad, or a large cheese platter. Can also be served with the sweet onion and bacon bread or cumin bread from recipes on pages 134 and 135.

Degree of difficulty: **Easy**
Preparation time: **45 minutes**

Kitchen equipment:
2 qt. pot
Blender or immersion blender
Sauté pan

Ingredients:
1 lb. (500 g) endives
4 tbsp. (55 g) butter
1 potato, large
Salt and pepper
Nutmeg
3 cups (75 cl) milk
4 scallions
1 cup toasted croutons

INVIGORATING SOUPS

They are closest to traditional soups that feed both the body and heart. They are those that the lady of the house generously ladles out to her family, in a loving motherly way, from a large steaming soup tureen. That does not mean that all recipes offered here are rural or common. Some show a certain degree of sophistication. However, based on vegetables, meat, seafood, and eggs, complemented by their open sandwiches, they all have the same function—to delight the palate and invigorate anyone exhausted at the end of the day.

5

SPLIT PEA SOUP AND FLAT SAUSAGES

La soupe de pois cassés et ses attriaux

●

The Soup

In principle, split peas do not need to be soaked. Simply wash them several times in cold water.

Peel and cut the carrots, onions, and celery into small dice. In the 3 qt. pot sweat them in the butter. Add 1.5 quarts (1,5 l) of water, the split peas, chopped garlic, bouquet garni, chicken stock, salt, and pepper, cook 1 hour. Pass through the fine disk of a food mill.

Before serving, reheat, add the crème fraîche, possibly dilute with extra chicken stock if the soup is too thick.

The flat sausages

Chop the pork and all the offal, and mix with the spices, eggs, flour, finely chopped onion, garlic, and shallot. Add the chopped parsley and chervil, with the dash of brandy.

Wash the caul with tepid water, then with cold vinegar water. Drain, wipe it dry, and cut it into 4 in. (10 cm.) squares.

Shape small balls of the offal mixture. Wrap each into a caul square. Flatten with the palm of your hand. Cook and lightly brown in a frying pan over low heat about 10 minutes.

Serve with the pea soup, sliced bread, and mustard.

Split pea soup is a great classic. It is suggested here with flat pork offal sausages, a specialty from Haute-Savoie, and more specifically from the area of Thonon. It is even celebrated yearly at the fair of Thonon, on the first Thursday of September.

Degree of difficulty: **Easy for the soup, more difficult for the flat sausages.**
Preparation time: **Soup: 1¾ hours Sausages: 45 minutes (prepared while the soup is cooking).**

Kitchen equipment:
3 qt. pot
Food mill with a fine disk
For the flat sausages:
A chef's knife or cleaver
Mixing bowl
Frying pan

Ingredients:
For the soup:
1 lb. (500 g) split peas
1 each: carrot, onion, celery stalk
2 tbsp. (30 g) butter
2 garlic cloves
1 bouquet garni
3 tbsp. chicken stock
¾ cup (20 cl) crème fraîche
For the flat sausages:
1 lbs. 10 oz. (750 g) pork
offal in the following proportions:
5 oz. (150 g) heart, 5 oz. (150 g) kidney, 8 oz. (225 g) jowl, 8 oz. (225 g) liver
1 tsp. each *quatre épices*, nutmeg, salt, and pepper
1 whole egg
1 tbsp. mustard
1 cup (150 g) flour
1 each: onion, garlic clove, shallot
Parsley and chervil
1 dash brandy or Savoy marc brandy
1 pork caul, large

Serves 5 to 6

Pulse soup lovers will also adore the CREAM OF GREEN DU PUY LENTIL SOUP AND COARSE *SABODET* STRIPS *Crème de lentilles vertes du puy et gros lardons de sabodet* This recipe is from a great chef, Christian Tetedoie, restaurateur in Lyon.

Wash the lentils thoroughly and soak in water for 3 hours.

One hour before the end of the lentils' soaking, cook the following in 2 quarts (2 l) of water: carrot, onion studded with the cloves, bouquet garni, and garlic. Simmer 1 hour.

At the end of the hour, add the lentils and cook 20 minutes. Add the light cream, return to the heat and simmer for 20 more minutes. Remove the vegetable garnish and, with a blender, purée the lentils with their bouillon.

Meanwhile, cook the *sabodet* for 25 minutes in water, cut it into thick strips and sauté in a frying pan.

Serve the cream of lentil soup very frothy, placing the coarse *sabodet* strips on it, and decorate with a dollop of sour cream and some chopped chervil.

Degree of difficulty: **Easy**
Preparation time: **50 minutes,**
3 hours for soaking lentils

Kitchen equipment:
3 qt. pot
Blender or immersion blender
Frying pan

Ingredients:
1½ cups (250 g) green lentils
    (du Puy)
1 carrot
1 onion
2 cloves
1 bouquet garni
4 garlic cloves
1 cup (2,5 dl) light cream
1 *sabodet* (pork head sausage, a
    specialty from Condrieu, France)
2 tbsp. sour cream
Chervil

STEWING HEN SOUP AND MEATBALLS

La soupe de poule et ses boulettes

●

Put the brain to soak in cold water with 2 tbsp. of vinegar.

Place the stewing hen into the stockpot, cover it with 4 quarts (4 l) of cold water. Add the veal bone, bouquet garni, onion studded with a clove, and crushed garlic clove, slowly bring to a boil.

Meanwhile, clean and wash all vegetables. Peel the carrots and rutabaga, string celery, cut in large sticks; tie the leeks into a bundle, and shred the swiss chard. After the hen bouillon boils, skim it, bring to a boil again, add the vegetables, salt, pepper, and *quatre épices*. The stewing should be done in about 1½ hours.

Start making the meatballs. Drain the brain, and wash it, remove any blood that did not dissolve, and take off the skin that covers it. Place it in a small pot with water, parsley, and lemon juice. Poach over low heat for 15 minutes, rinse under cold water and drain again.

Remove the breast meat from the cooked stewing hen; return the remaining meat to the stockpot with the vegetables, keep warm over low heat.

Grind the brain, veal, and white hen meat in a meat grinder with a fine disk. Place the parsley, egg yolk, and flour into a mixing bowl. Moisten the breadcrumbs with the milk, thoroughly press to wring it, crumble it, and thoroughly combine the mixture until you have a paste. If needed, add a little flour. Transfer about 2 quarts (2 l) of bouillon to the pot, bring to a simmer. Using two spoons, shape the into walnut-sized meatballs, poach for

Another soup with vegetables and protein that is a one-pot meal and very original. Its preparation requires some care; however, if you have a large table of guests with somewhat empty stomachs, their pleasure will justify the little effort required to prepare it.

Degree of difficulty: **Moderate**
Preparation time: **3 hours, cooking time included**

Kitchen equipment:
Stockpot
Meat grinder with fine disk
Mixing bowls
3 qt. pot

Ingredients:
For the bouillon:
1 stewing hen
1 veal bone
1 bouquet garni
1 onion, studded with a clove
1 garlic clove
3 carrots
1 rutabaga, small
2 celery stalks
6 leeks
3 swiss chard leaves
Salt and pepper
1 pinch *quatre épices*
For the meatballs:
1 calf brain
2 tbsp. white vinegar
Hen breast meat
5 oz. (150 g) veal top round
1 tbsp. parsley, chopped
2 egg yolks
2 tbsp. flour
1 cup dry breadcrumbs
3 tbsp. milk

10 minutes in the bouillon, drain, and keep warm over low heat.

Thin down the remaining egg yolk with a ladle of bouillon. Pour into the bouillon, stir over very low heat, do not boil.

Arrange the meatballs in the soup tureen, cover with the hot bouillon and separately serve the remaining stewing hen, carved, together with all vegetables.

●

Variation of this meatball soup:
KRASSENS SOUP, a specialty from Belle-Île, France.
La soupe aux krassens
Krassens are a kind of dough-quenelles.

Prepare the stewing hen bouillon as for the preceding recipe.

Pour the flour into a mixing bowl, make a well, break the eggs and drop them into it, add salt, pepper, and mix. Mix the yeast with a tbsp. of tepid water. Add to the dough, knead and let rest for 2 hours while the stewing hen is cooking.

Fill a pot with bouillon. Using a tablespoon, shape balls with the dough and cook them for 20 minutes in this bouillon.

Transfer a ladle of bouillon to a small saucepot, off the heat, thin down one egg yolk in it. Stir over low heat, paying attention not to boil it, add it to the cooking bouillon.

Serve this bouillon with the carved stewing hen, vegetables, and *krassens*.

Ingredients:
In addition to the ingredients and kitchen equipment required for the stewing hen bouillon, plan for:
3⅓ cups (500 g) flour
6 eggs
Salt and pepper
½ tsp. dried yeast

PORCINI MUSHROOM CASSEROLE AND GIZZARD CONFITS SANDWICHES

La mitonnée de cèpes et ses tartines de gésiers confits

Serves 4

●

Avoid washing porcini mushrooms. It is better to carefully brush them, if necessary briefly clean them under running water.

In the 2 qt. pot melt the butter, add 4 chopped shallots, and sweat 2 to 3 minutes. Add the diced mushrooms and bay leaf, simmer covered for 10 minutes, cover with 3 cups (75 cl) water and cook another 10 minutes.

Thoroughly combine the heavy cream with the bouillon, purée the mixture with a blender, correct seasoning, and keep warm.

Using a food processor, purée the gizzards together with their fat, to obtain a thick spread. Cover the toasted bread slices with it and sprinkle with the remaining minced raw shallot.

When the porcini mushrooms are picked, enjoying them is a must. So, on a nice fall day, you will take your basket and leisurely walk to the underwood. From these magnificent porcini mushrooms, you will prepare this savory casserole that you will accompany with open gizzard confits sandwiches, which gives it a typical fragrant touch from the southwest of France. If you do not pick the porcini mushrooms yourself, but buy them very fresh and firm from the market, the casserole will be as good; however, you may not be as hungry.

Degree of difficulty: **Easy**
Preparation time: **30 minutes**

Kitchen equipment:
2 qt. pot
Blender or immersion blender
Frying pan
Food processor

Ingredients:
2¼ lbs. (1 kg) porcini mushrooms
4 tbsp. (55 g) butter
6 shallots
1 bay leaf
1 cup (25 cl) heavy cream
Salt and pepper
4 to 8 gizzard confits, depending on appetites
Large country bread slices, toasted

OXTAIL SOUP WITH BULGUR

La soupe de queue de boeuf au boulghour

Serves 4

●

Tie the oxtail sections into bundles. Place them, together with the bouquet garni, into a stockpot filled with cold water. Bring to a boil over high heat, reduce heat and simmer 1¼ hours. During this time, the bouillon must be skimmed several times.

Clean and wash all vegetables. Peel the tomatoes, turnips, and carrots. Cut the celery stalk into small sections, quarter the tomatoes, cut and tie the leeks, and remove the outside skin from the garlic head without separating or peeling the cloves. Put all vegetables and garlic into the bouillon, add the ground chili and some salt. Continue cooking over low heat for 45 minutes.

Pour the bulgur wheat into a strainer and rinse thoroughly under cold water.

Using a skimmer, remove the cooked meat and vegetables from the stockpot. Strain the bouillon. Return it to the stockpot, bring to a boil again, slowly pour the bulgur into it, stir, cover and cook over low heat for 20 minutes.

Finally, add the meat and vegetables, reheat the soup for 5 minutes and serve at once.

This soup may be served as is, or serve the bouillon with bulgur in a soup tureen, the meat and vegetables on a separate serving dish.

This is the thriftiest and most complete of dishes, since it combines meat, vegetables, and grain. Furthermore, it stems from our local rural tradition, with inspiration from African cuisine; this simple fusion gives it an original taste. No matter how ravenously hungry your guests may be, you can bet that they will not be hungry anymore once they have finished this meal.

Degree of difficulty: **Easy**
Preparation time: **3 hours, cooking time included**

Kitchen equipment:
Stockpot
Kitchen string
Skimmer
Fine china cap
Strainer

Ingredients:
1 oxtail, sectioned
1 bouquet garni
2 tomatoes
2 white turnips
3 carrots
1 celery stalk
2 leeks
1 garlic bulb
½ tsp. chili, ground
Salt
1⅓ cups (200 g) bulgur wheat

CABBAGE SOUP
AND STUFFED PACKETS

La soupe au chou et ses petits farcis

Serves 6

●

Wash the cabbage. Remove the nicest large leaves for the packets and reserve. Shred the cabbage heart and blanch it for 2 minutes in boiling salted water. Rinse under cold water and pat dry.

Peel and dice the carrots and potatoes. Clean and wash the leeks, use only the white part, cut into slices.

Finely chop 1 onion, the shallots, and garlic cloves, sauté them in some of the confit fat. Add 1½ quarts (1,5 l) of boiling water, the vegetables, bouquet garni, the second onion studded with a clove, salt, and pepper. Cook 30 minutes.

Meanwhile, start preparing the wraps.

Blanch the reserved cabbage leaves in boiling salted water for 3 minutes. Drain, briefly hold under cold running water, and thoroughly pat dry. Lay them out on a cutting board and halve them, removing the central rib.

For the filling, peel the onion, shallots, and garlic; chop them with the parsley. Sauté in a little confit fat.

Remove the skin from the confit of duck wing and cut into small very thin small slices, also slice the gizzards. Add the onion, shallot, garlic, chopped parsley, season with salt and pepper, mix thoroughly.

Place a spoonful of filling into each half-leaf. Fold up like an envelope to make small packets; tie together with kitchen string.

How to turn a pleasant country cabbage soup into a sumptuous one-pot meal, by adding wraps with confit filling. It requires some time; however, you can certainly find some young kitchen help willing to assist you to stuff the confit into the cabbage leaves. Since this dish may very well be reheated at the last moment, you won't have to be afflicted with stress. Preparing it ahead of time makes it easy.

Degree of difficulty: **Moderate**
Preparation time: **1 hour**

Kitchen equipment:
Large stewpot
Pot
Chef's knife or a cleaver
Kitchen string

Ingredients:
1 green cabbage, large
1 lb. (500 g) carrots
1 lb. (500 g) potatoes
2 leeks, thick stemmed
2 onions
2 shallots
2 garlic cloves
Confit fat
1 bouquet garni
1 clove
Salt and pepper
For the packets:
1 small onion
2 shallots
2 garlic cloves
1 small bunch flat leaf parsley
1 confit of duck wing
8¾ oz. (250 g) confit of goose or
    duck gizzards
Salt and pepper

After the soup cooks for 30 minutes, carefully drop the packets into it. Cover and cook another 15 minutes over very low heat.

When serving, sprinkle the packets with minced parsley and accompany with sliced toasted country bread or perhaps homemade sweet onion and bacon bread (recipes on pages 132 and 135).

●

Serves 4

SAUERKRAUT SOUP, a specialty from Belle-Île, France.
La soupe a la choucroute

Place the sauerkraut into a colander and rinse it under water. Drain. Melt the butter in the 3 qt. pot, braise the sauerkraut in it and then add the thoroughly washed potatoes, onion, Alsatian tongue, juniper berries, and peppercorns.

Pour the chicken stock into the pot and simmer for about 1¾ hours.

Serve with bread, such as sweet onion and bacon bread or cumin bread (recipes on pages 134 and 135), toasted in the oven.

For cabbage soup lovers, a typically Alsatian version, the preferred dish of Dr. Schweitzer.

Degree of difficulty: **Easy**
Preparation time: **2 hours**

Kitchen equipment:
Colander
3 qt. stewpot
Grater

Ingredients:
14 oz. (400 g) sauerkraut
3 tbsp. (40 g) butter
2 large potatoes, coarsely grated
1 onion, chopped
4 slices Alsatian tongue sausage
   (*Zungenwurst*), thickly sliced
8 juniper berries
8 peppercorns
1½ quarts (1,5 l) chicken stock

FOR A FRUGAL MEAL, TWO CLEVER RECIPES

Et pour un repas improvisé, deux recettes à malice

INVENTIVE: CRAB SOUP AND POACHED EGGS
Inventive: la soupe au crabe et ses oeufs pochés

In the twinkling of an eye, clean and wash the leeks, peel and seed the tomatoes, peel the onion and garlic. Lightly brown these vegetables in oil, add 2 quarts (2 l) of water, thyme, bay, saffron, salt and pepper, cook for 10 to 15 minutes in a pressure cooker, or 30 to 40 minutes in a 3 qt. pot.

Meanwhile, drain the crab, remove any shell, add the crab to the vegetable bouillon after the vegetables are cooked and keep warm.

Cut small bread rounds. Poach the eggs in boiling vinegar water and toast the bread at the same time.

Serve the saffron bouillon in a soup tureen and the poached eggs on the toasts on warm dinner plates.

PROVIDING A CHANGE OF SCENE: SOUP *À L'INDIENNE* WITH SWEET AND SALTY GARNISH
Dépaysante: la soupe a l'indienne et sa garniture sucrée-salée

Prepare the curry cream according to the directions on the package. Before serving, add the crème fraîche and the curry powder to taste.

Serve this soup hot with the diced pineapple, and the peeled and diced apples. Sprinkle with lemon juice, shredded coconut, roasted almonds, raisins, and diced chicken meat.

It may happen that guests arrive without notice. Here are two express recipes that taste good and look nice.

CRAB SOUP AND
POACHED EGGS
Degree of difficulty: **Easy**
Preparation time: **25 minutes if you use a pressure cooker**

Kitchen equipment:
Pressure cooker or 3 qt. pot

Ingredients:
**8 leeks, white part only
2 tomatoes, 1 onion, 1 garlic clove
5 tbsp. oil
Some thyme, 1 bay leaf, 1 small
    tube or pinch of saffron
Salt and pepper
1 lb. lump crabmeat
6 eggs
1 French baquette**

SOUP *À L'INDIENNE* WITH
SWEET AND SALTY GARNISH
Degree of difficulty: **Easy**
Preparation time: **15 minutes**

Kitchen equipment:
2 qt. pot

Ingredients:
**2 packs Knorr curry cream
7 tbsp. (100 g) crème fraîche
1 tsp. curry powder
½ can pineapple, 2 large apples
1 lemon, ¾ cup (100 g) shredded
    coconut, ¾ cup (100 g) ground
    almonds, 1½ cups (250 g)
    raisins
11 oz. (300 g) white chicken meat,
    cooked**

FROM AFTERNOON TEA TO DESSERT

In the same way a good meal would be incomplete if not ended with the delights of dessert, something would be missing from our celebration of soups if sweet dishes were absent. So here are some, as delicious as they are easy to prepare, most based on fruit, a few on chocolate, for the winter months and chocolate lovers. As much as with fruitcakes, madeleines, and other small cakes, guests can gather around these soups for a sumptuous afternoon tea. They are also highly recommended if, adopting a clever North European and Anglo-Saxon custom, the traditional dinner invitation is substituted with an invitation to have . . . an after-dinner soup. Finally, they all have the advantage of being prepared long enough in advance.

6

RED WINE APPLE SOUP

Soupe de pommes en chabrot

●

Put the wine, sugar, cinnamon, and vanilla into the pot, boil over high heat, about 10 minutes.

Peel the apples and cut balls from them, using the large side of the melon baller.

Drop the apple balls into the red wine; avoid placing them on top of each other, thus the need for a wide pot.

Poach in the simmering liquid for 5 to 7 minutes; the apples have to be cooked but still firm.

Remove the pot from the heat and let steep about ten hours, stirring gently from time to time, until the apple balls take on a deep red color.

This soup is even more delicious when accompanied by a scoop of vanilla ice cream.

Its originality: Apples are cut into balls about the size of cherries. Its subtlety: Combination of flavors from the wine, cinnamon, and vanilla. Its presentation: a glass dish and for the iridescent effect, a "tablecloth" made from inexpensive fabric, but shiny and transparent, laid on a colored background.

Degree of difficulty: **Easy**
Preparation time: **20 minutes, but made ten hours in advance**

Kitchen equipment:
**Wide and heavy bottomed pot
Melon baller**

Ingredients:
**2¼ lbs. (1 kg) apples (preferably maygold or russet), any type that will remain firm when cooked
1 pint (½ l) red wine
1¼ cup (250 g) sugar
1 cinnamon stick
1 vanilla bean pod, split**

Serves 4

CHILLED SOUP OF PEACHES WITH RED CURRANT JUICE

La soupe glacée de pêches au jus de groseille

Serves 4

●

Slowly melt the sugar in water and bring to a boil, to make a syrup. Let cool.

Pick off the red currants, purée and strain them. Combine the syrup with the lemon juice and pour into the currant juice.

Peel the peaches, cut them into wedges. Arrange them in a salad bowl, add the red currant syrup, decorate with the mint leaves and chill in the refrigerator till ready to serve. Chill.

Unlike the red wine apple soup on page 110, this can only be prepared in the summer months, with fresh and fully matured fruit. The two in duo create a gourmet feast!

Degree of difficulty: **Easy**
Preparation time: **30 minutes, plus 1 hour chilling**

Kitchen equipment:
1½ qt. pot
Food processor
Strainer
Salad bowl

Ingredients:
6 large white peaches
1⅓ cups (300 g) red currants
1 cup (200 g) sugar
1 cup (¼ l) water
Juice of 1 lemon
A few mint leaves

RHUBARB, STRAWBERRY, AND MINT SOUP

Soupe de rhubarbe, fraises et menthe

Serves 4

●

Put the water, sugar, vanilla bean pod, cinnamon, and mint, reserving a few mint leaves, into a pot. Slowly melt the sugar and briefly bring to the boil.

Clean the rhubarb and cut into ¾ in. (2 cm) dice. Drop into the boiling syrup, briefly bring to a boil again, remove from the heat at once; the rhubarb must stay a little firm, without becoming soft. Transfer to a salad bowl, let steep and cool down.

Finally, add the strawberries. Before serving, remove the cooked mint leaves, and decorate with some fresh mint.

The combination of rhubarb and strawberries is a delight to the taste buds. During the so short—but so great—rhubarb season, don't miss this perfect match. And see how well the green glazed bowl complements its color.

Degree of difficulty: **Easy**
Preparation time: **30 minutes**

Kitchen equipment:
Pot
Salad bowl

Ingredients:
3⅓ lbs. (1,5 kg) rhubarb
14 oz. (400 g) strawberries
2 quarts (2 l) water
2 cups (400 g) sugar
1 vanilla bean pod, split
1 cinnamon stick
1 bunch mint

ALMOND MILK AND STRAWBERRY SOUP

La soupe au lait d'amandes et aux fraises

Serves 4

●

Prepare the almond milk by bringing the milk and all other ingredients, except the strawberries, to a boil.

Steep for 15 minutes, pour through a fine china cap, thoroughly pressing the ingredients through, and let cool down.

Halve the strawberries and add to the milk, place in the refrigerator. Serve this soup chilled.

Almonds and strawberries, another ideal combination. If you serve this for a children's afternoon snack, it will be a resounding triumph. Therefore, think big!

Degree of difficulty: **Easy**
Preparation time: **25 minutes**

Kitchen equipment:
Pot
Fine china cap
Salad bowl or glass dish

Ingredients:
1²/₃ cups (40 cl) milk
1 cup (50 g) ground almonds
¹/₂ cup (100 g) sugar
1 vanilla bean pod, split
4 tbsp. maraschino liquor
1 lb. (500 g) strawberries, hulled

CHERRY AND FLAVORED RED WINE SOUP

Soupe de cerises au vin rouge aromatisé

Serves 6 to 8

●

Pit the cherries.

Put the wine and citrus peel into a pot, reduce by half, then add the sugar, tea, port wine, and cherries and boil for 5 minutes.

Remove the cherries and tea bags, add the pepper and sticks of licorice, and thicken with cornstarch dissolved in 3 tbsp. of water. Boil again for 5 minutes. Let cool.

Add the cherries and serve chilled.

With this soup, cherry season takes on a new flavor: tea and licorice bring it an unusual touch. Guessing game: Ask your guests to speculate what the flavors are. As for decoration, this original dish is served in an unusual container: a glass flowerpot.

Degree of difficulty: **Easy**
Preparation time: **30 minutes**

Kitchen equipment:
4 qt. pot
Cherry pitter

Ingredients:
4½ lbs. (2 kg) cherries
3 quarts (3 l) red wine
1 orange peel, grated
1 lemon peel, grated
2½ cups (500 g) sugar
2 teabags, Earl Grey type
1 pint (0,5 l) port wine
1 tbsp. cornstarch
1½ tbsp. (20 g) black pepper
3 oz. (80 g) licorice sticks

CHOCOLATE VELOUTÉ WITH FLOATING ISLANDS

Velouté de chocolat aux îles flottantès

Serves 6

●

First prepare the snowy islands that will "float" on the chocolate velouté. To do this, separate the egg whites from the egg yolks. Reserve the egg yolks.

Whisk the egg whites till stiff in a mixing bowl, gradually adding 1½ cups (300 g) of sugar.

Butter the small ramekins. Fill each with beaten egg whites. Bake a few minutes in a 350°F (180°C) oven. To check for doneness, carefully touch the egg whites; if they do not stick, the "islands" are ready.

For the chocolate velouté, put the milk and split vanilla bean pod into a pot and bring to the boil. Subsequently add the chocolate in small chunks. Stir.

Whisk the egg yolks with the remaining ½ cup (100 g) of sugar, until they lighten. Transfer them to a second pot, gradually add the chocolate milk while stirring, and cook the contents, as you cook custard, stirring constantly.

At the last moment, add the cold espresso.

Pour this velouté into serving dishes, float the meringue islands on top and serve . . . while dancing if you want.

A winter dessert, a Christmas afternoon tea, and a moment of intense gratification for those who both have a passion for chocolate and the nostalgia for their grandmothers' floating islands.

Degree of difficulty: **Moderate**
Preparation time: **45 minutes**

Kitchen equipment:
Two mixing bowls
Wire whisk
6 individual ovenproof ramekins
2 qt. pots

Ingredients:
12 eggs
1¼ qt. (1¼ l) milk
11 oz. (300 g) bittersweet chocolate
1 vanilla bean pod, split
1 cup cold espresso
2 cups (400 g) granulated sugar

FRESH FRUIT MINESTRONE

Minestrone de fruits frais

Serves 6

●

Put the water, sugar, lime peel, basil leaves, and vanilla bean pod with seeds scraped into the pot. Slowly dissolve the sugar and bring to a boil.

Once the contents have boiled, remove from the heat and let steep for 30 minutes. Strain, add the apricot juice, and reserve in the refrigerator.

Peel and cut all fruit into a ¼ in. (½ cm) dice. Pour the apricot syrup into the serving dish. Add the fruit dice. Decorate with a few minced basil leaves, and if possible, a few field strawberries.

Serve chilled, perhaps with a scoop of lime sorbet.

It is really difficult to dream of something more refreshing, simpler or more appetizing to look at. It's the whole summer in a bowl.

Degree of difficulty: **Easy**
Preparation time: **1 hour**

Kitchen equipment:
Pot
Strainer

Ingredients:
14 oz. (400 g) water
⅓ cup (70 g) granulated sugar
1 piece of lime peel
6 basil leaves
1 vanilla bean pod, split
1¾ cups (400 g) apricot juice
1 banana
3 apricots
1 white peach
1 mango
1 kiwi fruit
8 to 10 strawberries
½ papaya (these fruits are not mandatory—depending on the season, substitute some fruit; the important thing is the combination)

CHOCOLATE SOUP AND PINEAPPLE

Soupe au chocolat et à l'ananas

●

Break the chocolate into pieces and pour the hot milk over it. As soon as a shiny texture is obtained, stir to create a homogenous mix, stir in the cold milk, and place into the refrigerator overnight or longer.

Cut the skin from the pineapple and cut into thin slices.

Put the water, sugar, and star anise into the pot. Slowly melt the sugar and bring to a boil. Pour this boiling syrup on the pineapple and let marinate overnight in the refrigerator.

To serve, lay the cake croutons on a baking sheet. Sprinkle them with confectioners' sugar and toast them under a broiler till golden brown and crisp.

Drain the pineapple slices; divide them among small bowls or glass dishes, surround with the chocolate soup and top with warm croutons.

The magic cocoa bean and juicy pineapple both originate in the tropics. Marry them, and you will see how well they complement each other—making an amusing presentation.

Degree of difficulty: **Easy**
Preparation time: **30 minutes plus overnight for marinating**

Kitchen equipment:
Pot
Mixing bowl

Ingredients:
1¼ lb. (1 kg) milk chocolate bars
1¾ cups (400 g) hot milk
⅞ cup (200 g) cold milk
1 ripe pineapple
2 cups (0,5 l) water
¾ cup (150 g) sugar
2 star anise pods
For the croutons, a sponge cake, or pound cake cut in small dice

Serves 6

EXOTIC FRUIT SOUP

La soupe de fruits exotiques

Serves 6 to 8

●

Place the water, sugar, spices, vanilla, zests, lemongrass, and minced mint into the 2 qt. pot. Heat slowly to dissolve the sugar. Stir well, boil for 5 minutes, remove from the heat, let steep, and cool.

Peel and dice the mango and the pineapple. Peel and slice the kiwi fruits, and put the passion fruits aside.

When the syrup has cooled, strain it through a fine china cap, transfer it to a serving bowl with the cut fruits, cut and add the passion fruit pulp and seeds to the bowl.

Place in refrigerator for 3 hours to chill. Add fresh chopped mint before serving.

It is sunshine for cold days; colors to brighten a gray day. A change of taste for tired palates and a light dessert to finish a meal on a reggae note.

Degree of difficulty: **Easy**
Preparation time: **30 minutes plus 3 hours for chilling**

Kitchen equipment:
2 qt. pot
Fine china cap
Serving bowl

Ingredients:
1 qt. (1 l) water
¾ cup (150 g) sugar
1 clove
½ tsp. Chinese five spice
1 tsp. fresh ginger, chopped
3 coriander seeds
1½ vanilla bean pods, split
2 lime zests
1 lemon zest
1½ bunches fresh lemon grass, coarsely chopped
1 tbsp. minced mint
1 mango
1 pineapple
8 kiwi fruits
12 passion fruits
1 bunch fresh mint

CANDIED FIGS AND *BEAUME DE VENISE* MUSCATEL WINE SOUP

Soupe au muscat de beaume de venise et figues confites

●

Serves 6

Pour the muscatel wine into the sauté pan. Add the honey and both fennels. Bring to a boil.

Wash and dry the figs. Prick them with a needle. Drop into the wine and stew 20 minutes on low heat.

Remove the figs and drain. Reduce the soup by half, add back the figs, and remove from the heat.

Cool and place in the refrigerator overnight.

Based on alcohol, this soup is for adults only. It is more than likely that with it they will end the day in a bubble of lightness.

Degree of difficulty: **Easy**
Preparation time: **1 hour, and 1 day ahead**

Kitchen equipment:
Large sauté pan
Colander
Serving bowl

Ingredients:
1 bottle *Beaume de Venise* muscatel wine
⅔ cup (200 g) honey
1 tsp. (10 g) fennel seeds
1 tsp. (10 g) ground fennel
2¼ lbs. (1 kg) green figs, fresh

BREAD AND OILS

Bread is soaked in the soup . . . or served as savory open sandwiches. A dash of flavored oils adds spirit to the soup. For this work to be complete, Léni Chevasson, the great innkeeper of the hotel-restaurant *Le Tilleul* in Générargues in the Cévennes (France), gave us her bread recipes, and Michel Bras, the great chef from Laguiole (France), the secret of his flavored oils.

THE BREADS THAT COMPLEMENT THE SOUPS

Les pains qui vont avec

●

To accompany these soups, and *potages*, there is nothing like plain or toasted bread, or sliced cake made to complement salty dishes. Léni Chevasson, the great innkeeper from the hotel-restaurant *Le Tilleul* in Générargues, Cévennes (France), only serves breads that she hand-kneads and bakes herself. They are exceptional. For your soup dinners, she enriches the range even further.

Degree of difficulty: **Moderate**
Preparation time: **About 3 hours, to prep, raise and bake**

Kitchen equipment:
Two mixing bowls, one very large
A piece of oilcloth
Long metal or plastic spatula
Pastry board
Large piece of cheesecloth
Parchment paper
Baking sheet

Ingredients:
For a large bread about 2 lbs. (1 kg)
7½ cups bread flour (or mixed
    white and whole-wheat flour)
3 cups (75 cl) water
2 tsp. (10 g) salt
1 tbsp. dried yeast

COUNTRY BREAD
Le pain de campagne

Put the flour into the smaller mixing bowl; add the salt, and most of the tepid water 90°F (38° C) all at once, and then mix the yeast with the remaining tepid water. Knead it by hand or with a spatula, but not too much; the water should only be folded into the flour.

Transfer the dough to a large mixing bowl, cover it with the oilcloth; a warm humid and muggy place is required, the oilcloth keeps the humidity well. After about 1½ to 2 hours, the yeast will have done its work, a dough will be doubled or tripled in volume.

Remove the oilcloth, wash and dry it, place it on the pastry board to cover, generously sprinkle with flour. Using the spatula, lay the dough on it, sprinkle generously with flour. Still using the spatula, fold it two or three times and subsequently knead it by hand for a little while. Finally, shape the loaf in a round or rectangular.

Cover with the wet and wrung cheesecloth. Let rise for 20 to 30 minutes.

Meanwhile, preheat the oven to 400°F (200°C). Place the loaf on a parchment paper covered baking sheet and into the oven.

The bread is done when the crust is golden brown and a tip of a knife stuck into it comes out clean.

Makes a 2 lb. loaf

From this basic recipe, many breads that complement with the soups can be made.

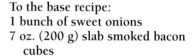

RED PEPPER BREAD
Le pain aux poivrons rouges

To the base recipe:
3 red peppers
2 tbsp. olive or walnut oil
1 pinch of oregano or savory

A great accompaniment to all cold soups such as gazpacho and cucumber soup, or with the minestrone and pesto soup.

Broil the peppers in the oven about 15 minutes to blister on all sides, place them in a closed container (peeling will be easier).

Just before shaping the loaf, cut the pepper into fine strips and fold into the dough with the herbs. Shape the loaf, raise, and bake in a 400°F (200°C) oven.

SWEET ONION AND BACON BREAD
Le pain au lard et aux oignons doux

To the base recipe:
1 bunch of sweet onions
7 oz. (200 g) slab smoked bacon cubes

A good companion of hearty, country style and vegetable soups, served in thick slices.

While the dough rises, peel and thinly slice the onions. Lightly brown them in a little oil or butter. Blanch the bacon cubes a few minutes in boiling water, drain, and fry to crisp. Fold into the dough before shaping the loaf.

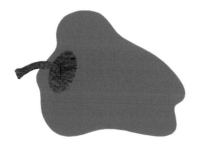

PAPRIKA AND CUMIN BREAD
Le pain au paprika et au cumin

To the base recipe:
2 tbsp. paprika
1 tbsp. cumin seeds

It really looks ethnic with hot or cold borscht and cream of asparagus soup. Also delicious with *fromage blanc* and mixed herbs.

Fold in the paprika and most of the cumin, shape the loaf and sprinkle the remaining cumin seeds before baking.

POPPY SEED BREAD
Le pain aux granies de pavot

To the base recipe:
½ cup (50 g) poppy seeds

Its very delicate flavor makes it a good companion for scrambled eggs, exotic soups, sweet and salty combinations.

Fold in most of the poppy seeds, and sprinkle the loaf with some poppy seeds and a little flour before baking.

OLIVE BREAD
Le pain aux olives

To the base recipe:
9 oz. (250 g) black pitted olives
Olive oil for brushing

It goes well with all Mediterranean flavors and mixed salads that may accompany the soups.

Coarsely chop the olives and fold into dough, shape the loaf and brush with olive oil before baking.

Before placing into the oven, pour a trickle of olive oil on the loaf.

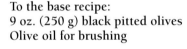

INSTEAD OF BREAD, CAKE FOR A CHANGE

Pour changer du pain, des cakes

Makes 1 cake

●

OLIVE CAKE
Cake aux olives

A pleasant accompaniment for soup or terrine or as an appetizer.

Combine all ingredients in the mixing bowl. Lightly oil the loaf pan. Bake at 400°F (200°C) for 30 minutes. The cake is done when tested with a knife the blade comes out clean.

Degree of difficulty: **Easy**
Preparation time: **1 hour**

Kitchen equipment:
Mixing bowl
Loaf pan

Ingredients:
1¾ cups (250 g) flour, sifted
4 large eggs
5 oz. (150 g) ham, small dice
7 tbsp. (1 dl) olive oil
7 tbsp. (1 dl) dry white wine
7 tbsp. (50 g) gruyère, grated
½ package dried yeast
4½ oz. (125 g) green olives, pitted

●

UNSWEETENED POUND CAKE
Le gâteau trois-tiers

In fact it is a pound cake without sugar, which has only three ingredients. It is to be spread with taramasalata or eggplant caviar, or to be soaked in fruit soup.

Put the flour into a mixing bowl, with salt and pepper. Add the melted butter, and thoroughly mix in the egg yolks (never the egg yolks before the butter, this will produce lumps), then fold in the stiffly beaten egg whites and saffron stigmas, for flavor and color.

Lightly butter the mold. Bake at 375°F (190°C) and 400°F about 30 minutes.

Degree of difficulty: **Easy**
Preparation time: **1 hour**

Kitchen equipment:
Mixing bowl
Loaf pan
Mixer

Ingredients:
1⅔ cups (250 g) flour, sifted
4 large eggs
2¼ sticks (250 g) melted butter
2 pinches salt and pepper
A few saffron stigmas (optional)

WHY NOT SOME BLINI?

Et pourquoi pas des blinis?

This recipe is a gift of Katia Guttmann, who once was the owner of the delicious small restaurant *Duna* in Paris, rue du Faubourg-Poissonnière. Quite a few food lovers have discovered the cuisine of Central Europe through Katia's cooking. These blini, when spread with taramasalata, salmon roe or smoked salmon, happily accompany seafood soups, scrambled eggs, etc.

●

Separate the whites from the egg yolks. Dissolve the yeast in a little milk or tepid water. Combine all ingredients except the egg whites in a mixing bowl to make a smooth batter, careful that it is not too liquid. Let rest at least 1 hour.

After this time, carefully fold in the stiffly beaten egg whites, let rest for another 15 minutes before cooking.

For this last step, coat the pan with a mixture of oil (preferably sunflower or grape seed) and melted butter. If a blini pan is not available, a large non-stick pan may be used by spooning several small "pools" of batter. The finish blini will be less perfect, however, the cooking will be faster.

Degree of difficulty: Moderate
Preparation time: 15 minutes for the batter plus 1¼ hours for rising. They may be prepared in advance, reheated in a warm oven, lightly buttered and wrapped in parchment paper.

Kitchen material:
Mixing bowl
Mixer
Blini pan or a large frying pan, preferably non-stick

Ingredients:
4 eggs
1¼ tsp. dried yeast
5 cups (750 g) flour
2 tbsp. sugar
Salt and ground pepper
2 to 3 tbsp. oil and butter
1 quart (1 l) milk, lukewarm

Serves 6

CATECHU OIL

L'huile de rocou

●

An amusing exotic one. Catechu, a powerful reddish-brown coloring, is extracted from the areca nut and is none other than the betel, so popular in India. Black slaves from the Antilles used it to paint their faces and bodies. In France, it's called "cachou"; it is indeed one of the main ingredients of a famous candy. One of my friends makes a lightly pigmented oil from it. She coats her roasts, peps up her vegetables, and spices up her vinaigrettes with it.

The recipe is limited to one gesture; drop the catechu into a peanut oil bottle, shake well to mix; replace the oil and a little catechu to the bottle. It is always useful to have it handy.

Gift boxes of assorted condiments offered by stores are appreciated gifts. Be even more original with homemade flavored oils that cannot be found in stores. A little sprinkle to your soups will add a nice subtle flavor to them.

Degree of difficulty: **Easy**
Preparation time: **Instantaneous**

Ingredients:
1 tsp. **Catechu, also called cashoo (in specialty spice stores)**
1 cup (25 cl) **peanut oil**

MICHEL BRAS' "SAVORY PEARLS"

Les "perles de saveur" de Michel Bras

Michel Bras, the great chef from Laguiole (France), in the Aubrac region, with three stars in the Michelin red guide, creates superb flavored oils that notably accompany his amazing vegetable dishes. He generously authorized us to reveal their alchemy. Choose the flavor to harmonize with the recipe you prepare.

●

PARSLEY OIL
Huile de persil

Sort and wash the parsley, eliminate large stems (that may be used in a stock for the soup). Purée the parsley with a little oil and a pinch of salt. Strain through a fine strainer. Let steep for about 4 hours and bottle.

In the same way, other flavored oils, for instance chive oil, may be prepared, with ¾ cup (50 g) of chives, to ⅓ cup (8 cl) of oil. Scallions or lovage (an ancient plant that is popular again, and has the same fragrance as celery, but more subtle and finer) may also be used.

At Michel Bras', parsley oil notably dots the plate of a sumptuous vegetable dish, the *gargouillou*. The chive oil flirts with a warm salmon fillet.

Degree of difficulty: **Easy**
Preparation time: **20 minutes plus 4 hours of patience**

Kitchen equipment:
Blender
Fine strainer

Ingredients:
2⅓ cups (150 g) flat leaf parsley
1 cup (25 cl) grape seed oil
Salt

●

WILD THYME OIL
Huile de serpolet

Remove any impurities from the wild thyme flowers. Immerse them into a glass jar filled with oil, let steep in the sun for a few days. Michel Bras plays magically with it, combining it with braised lobster and fresh wild thyme.

Ingredients:
1 bunch wild thyme flowers
⅓ cup (10 cl) olive oil

Makes 1 cup of oil

ST. JOHN'S WORT OIL
Huile de millepertuis

Pick enough St. John's wort flowers to fill a glass jar. Cover with grape seed oil and let steep in the sun a few days, shaking from time to time. Once the oil turns red, it is ready to use. Along with its flavor, it is known for healing stomachaches. Michel Bras makes a vinaigrette that he serves with a calf's liver, pink inside, and an extraordinary salad of valeriana phu (that may be substituted with mache salad) and ice plant (also called crystalline).

Ingredients:
A jar of St. John's wort flowers
Grape seed oil

DANDELION OIL
Huile de pissenlit

Alchemy and chemistry. Fill a jar with plucked petals of dandelion flowers picked on a sunny day. Cover with grape seed oil. Let steep for 48 hours in the refrigerator and then strain several times through a fine strainer the bottom of which is sprinkled with magnesium sulfate. That is the great secret. The magnesium catches water molecules and the oil keeps longer while keeping its entire flavor. Used when deglazing the cooking juices, giving a sweet and sour saddle of rabbit an incredible flavor of dandelion flowers.

Ingredients:
A jar of dandelion flowers
Grape seed oil
Magnesium sulfate from the drugstore

SPICE OIL
Huile aux epices

It's a mixture of grape seed oil (an oil with a neutral taste) and essential oils of cinnamon, clove, and nutmeg. Recommended proportion: 1 drop of each of these oils for 5 tbsp. (7,5 cl) of grape seed oil. At Michel Bras' it is used, for example, to make an emulsion of leek greens that accompanies a pan seared pigeon breast served with leeks braised in a bit of water and butter.

Ingredients:
Essential oils of cinnamon, clove, and nutmeg
Grape seed oil

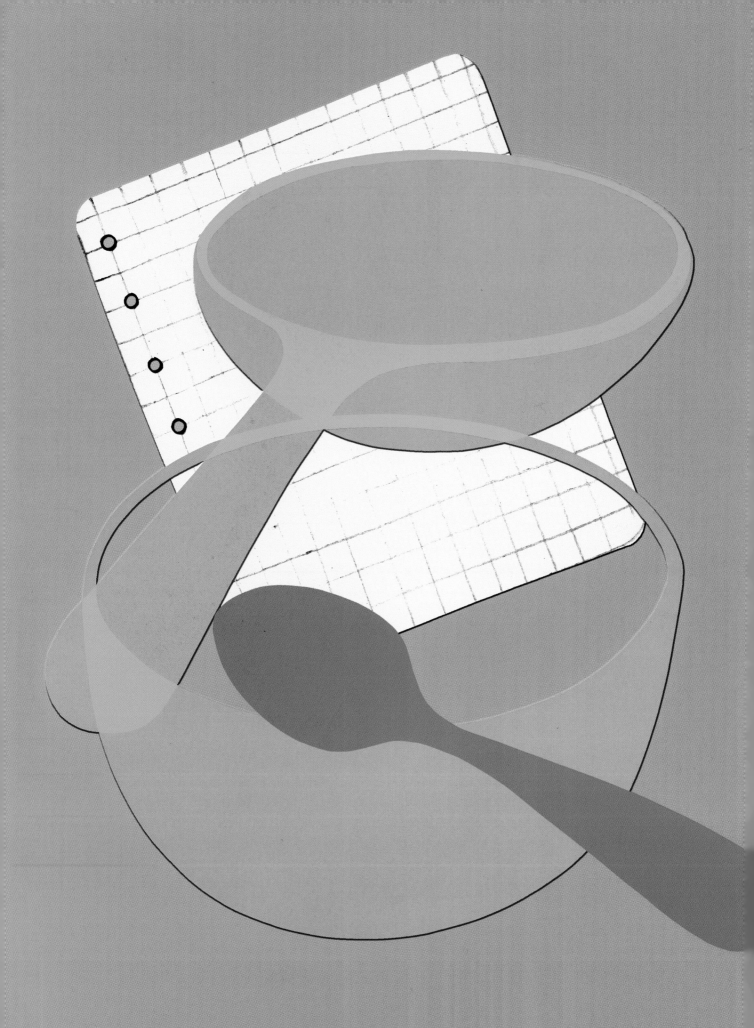

A LADLE OF EXPERIENCE

Whether it is called *potage*, consommé, soup, velouté, purée, or cream of this or that, it is always about a liquid food, of varying thickness, based on water or milk, enriched with nutritive additions. Generally served hot, sometimes cold—seemingly satisfied with its usual role as a starter for a meal—soup was for a long time the main course, the *pièce de résistance* for the poor. In this book we hope to restore soup to its status as centerpiece of the meal.

From *potage* to velouté

Throughout the centuries, with the gradual evolution of tastes, with the professionalization—going back to ancient times—of cooks, the vocabulary of soup preparation became diversified to a confusing degree. Although technical knowledge is in no way required in order to answer the craving for soup for dinner, it may be useful to clarify the origin of terms. Etymologically, the word "*potage*" pertains to foods cooked in a pot, and the word "soup" to preparations consisting of bread or various grains soaked in a liquid. Nowadays, the definitions have slightly changed. *Potages* come from two families: clear *potages* and thickened *potages*.

The clear *potages* are the most authentic descendants of the original definition of their name. In reality they are "consommés," that is, preparations based on water, vegetables, meat, and spices of various kinds, cooked long enough for the broth to become infused with the juices and fragrances of its ingredients. Preparations using lean beef or veal are called "white consommés." They may be served as a clear broth, or various ingredients may be added (meats, poultry, vegetables, pasta, quenelles, etc.). In the recipes that we are offering, consommés can also serve as the base for more elaborate *potages*, multiplying their taste tenfold. Sometimes they are to be served chilled.

Thickened *potages* have become more remote from their origin. They include cream soups, veloutés, purées, and porridge. They can be based on a simple white consommé, or on milk, the cooking water of a fresh vegetable, or even plain water. What is important and a basic characteristic of this kind of soup is the thickener: usually starch, grain (like rice), flour, or any purée. Bisque, a very sophisticated version of these thickened soups, belongs to this family. It is essentially a thinned purée, obtained by processing the cooked and peeled flesh of shellfish like lobster, crayfish, shrimp, crab, or langoustine, through a food mill. In many recipes for thickened *potages*, in the cream soup or velouté category, the addition of various ingredients like cornstarch, egg yolks, or crème fraîche enhance the thickening by adding smoothness.

Cream soups are based on clear consommé, the cooking water of the vegetable that will be the dominant flavor of the soup, or sometimes milk. Practically any vegetable can be turned into a cream soup: cauliflower, artichokes, celery, sorrel, green peas, asparagus, lettuce, and mushrooms are all suitable. The cooked vegetable is puréed very fine and added to a mixture based on a thickening agent (such as flour, cornstarch, or cream of rice) and a liquid in a process similar to preparing a Béchamel sauce (based on milk) or a white sauce (based on water or flavored bouillon). Once again, egg yolks and crème fraîche are called upon. The word "velouté" is used because it brings an image of velour (velvet) to mind. In reality, these soups belong either to the category of puréed *potage*, thickened by egg yolks, butter, or cream; or cream *potage*, made from a béchamel type base. They can be made from vegetables, poultry, mushrooms, etc.

What we consider to be dear old soups came to be referred to as *potage* in gastronomic vocabulary. Classic cookbooks generally define "soup" as cooked with water, sometimes with milk, containing various vegetables cut into pieces of varying sizes (corresponding to the "soaking bread"). Various beef stews and other stews are supposed to be part of this category, although if we are to be accurate etymologically, they correspond more closely to the original definition of *potage*. Could it be because—from these good stews of Auvergne to boiled chicken béarnaise—they have the same peasant stigma that sticks to soups with their soaked bread? Classification of culinary categories is sometimes confusing, and often does not make much sense.

Added flavor

Even though we are somewhat ignorant about what on earth ancient women were adding to their concoctions to make them more savory, there are enough texts from antiquity to provide evidence that for thousands of years they knew how to add flavor, often using ingredients that do not correspond to present day tastes. To the basic cooking ingredients, they added condiments, spices, and fragrant herbs.

Romans widely used garum and honey. Cooks in the Middle Ages called upon honey and spices (in odd combinations). Nowadays, with more discrimination, the use of aromatic plants and spices is incessantly fine-tuned. Apart from the great standards like garlic, onion, the inevitable bouquet garni with thyme, bay, parsley, chervil, clove, and celery stalk—or, even better, lovage (*levisticum oficinale*), which is more delicate—the gastronomic herbarium contains many more small marvels that are well suited for soups and *potages*, as long as one knows to measure them carefully and put them to good use. You will find a great number of them in the recipes in this book. On days you decide to make some improvisations, perhaps you might keep notes:

Juniper berries, which go so well with cabbage.

Nutmeg, an accessory of Béchamel sauce, purées, and pumpkin.

Quatre épices (allspice) that does not come from four plants but from only one. The ground fruit combines the flavors of clove, ginger, nutmeg, and pepper.

When grated, horseradish, closely matching the taste of black radish, enhances the flavor of a stew.

Ginger, often used for exotic Far East soups.

Saffron, a good companion to fish soups.

Sage, said to have digestive properties, where one leaf is enough to give pork a subtle flavor.

Dill and fennel, standards with fish based dishes.

Cumin, very popular in Alsatian cuisine; and paprika, often used in Central European soups.

Basil, of course—without it pesto soup would not exist.

In many cases, a dash of oil can also enrich the flavor of a consommé or *potage*. Depending on the ingredients used, it may be plain oil, olive oil, walnut oil, sesame oil—or even better, one of the flavored oils that the great chef from Laguiole (France), Michel Bras, authorized us to reveal the secrets of, found on pages 140 and 141.

Nutritious complements

Observation #1: Cooking in a liquid softens what is hard and improves what is barely edible. That is the justification for the pot and its *potage*. Observation #2: The liquid, as delicious as it may be, even with meat and vegetables, is not necessarily sufficient to fill empty stomachs. Grain in the form of bread, *galettes* (flat round cakes), and various pastas and dumplings make one-pot meals more nutritious. Very early in history, enhancements appeared. Not only giving the liquid meal some body, they also provide a kind of completeness and dietary balance. In addition to the mineral salts and vitamins from vegetables, they deliver much needed carbohydrates and proteins. The art of making flat corn cake was mastered in pre-Columbian America, where a formulary lists seven recipes. Incas thickened soups with quinoa and strongly spiced it with chili. In China, during the Han dynasty (about 200 B.C.), they knew all the secrets of rice noodles. In India, a kind of rice grits is added to fortify bouillons. Egyptians were quite successful preparing meats in a pot, hence *pot-au-feu* (stewed meat). Whether this stew is made with meat or poultry, it cannot be conceived without fava beans, lentils, and chickpeas. The Hebrews who later left the Pharaonic kingdom reminisced about these dishes for years. The more centuries go by, the greater the number of rediscovered enhancements—from the simplest to the most elaborate ones. They are still used today, and a good number of our recipes for dinner soups call upon them. For your improvised dishes, however, it may be useful to mention some suggestions:

Morsels or strips of salty crepes and blini.

All kinds of pasta, from vermicelli to the macaroni of pesto soup.

Profiteroles stuffed with a choice of fillings are excellent with consommés, veloutés, and certain soups.

Ravioli stuffed with green vegetables (spinach, swiss chard) and cheese.

All kinds of quenelles made from fish, meat, etc.

Finally, there is *milhas*, so dear to southern France. It is a kind of thick cornmeal mush similar to Italian polenta. When cool, it firms up into a cake from which slices can be cut, optionally pan seared, and added to various bouillons. Preparing *milhas* is a difficult matter, requiring a certain virtuosity to stir the mush for a long time, but excellent ready made *milhas* can be found in stores, vacuum packed or deep frozen.

A little advice

Vegetables

As good jams cannot be successfully made from spoiled or unripe fruit, good soups cannot be made from vegetables that are not fresh. If not picked from your garden the same day they are to be used, they should come from a good store—blemish free and ripe.

Say "no" to green and tasteless tomatoes, to yellowed leeks, to wilted greens, and to soft carrots. Keep your produce in the refrigerator, in the vegetable crisper . . . but not for too long.

Meat

Long cooking time enables the use of what is commonly known as "cheap cuts" that are, however, often tastier than cuts with a higher reputation—and are considerably thriftier. For beef, favor shin or shank, clod, oxtail, and cheek, if you like soft but a little gelatinous cuts. Choose brisket, *tendron* (rib end), and ribs, if you like fat meat cuts; shoulder and *macreuse* (a piece from the chuck), if you prefer leaner ones. A good soup contains a combination of two types of meat.

Veal is also classified into soft and lean. *Tendron* (rib end), flank, short rib, and knuckle are part of the first category. *Quasi* (a cut from the rump near the tail end) is leaner, but a bit dry to our taste—and considerably more expensive.

Lamb, always a little high in fat, is not recommended.

Pork is used either in the form of fresh meat like spare ribs, ham, loin, shoulder, and ribs, or in the form of slab bacon or salt pork.

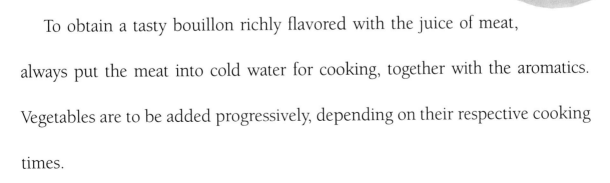

To obtain a tasty bouillon richly flavored with the juice of meat, always put the meat into cold water for cooking, together with the aromatics. Vegetables are to be added progressively, depending on their respective cooking times.

Potatoes should be cooked in some of the broth, but separately—otherwise they would make the bouillon cloudy.

Meat broth should always be skimmed as it comes to a boil, and it is often even better and more easily digested if the fat is skimmed off. If the broth is prepared well in advance so that it can be cooled, the fat will congeal on the surface and can easily be removed using a skimmer. Before serving, reheat an impeccable broth.

Some technical terms

Professional cooks have a vocabulary that often puzzles home cooks. We tried to avoid the jargon, since it is fairly easy to translate into everyday language. A few terms inevitably remain, however, and are defined as follows:

Blanch: Place a vegetable into boiling water for a few minutes to remove its bitterness, as with cabbage, or to quickly precook it. Generally, the blanched vegetable is cooled in cold water and dried thoroughly.

Brown: To cook in fat until the food becomes a golden brown color. To sauté is almost the same process; the only difference is that the meat or vegetable does not necessarily turn golden brown.

Clarify: To make a broth or bouillon fully clear by either straining it through

cheesecloth, or by simmering a few minutes with whisked egg white in it,

which will coagulate and catch suspended particles in the bouillon. It is

best to combine both methods, first the egg white, then the cheesecloth.

Crush: To grind coarsely.

Cut into brunoise: Cut into small even vegetable dice.

Cut into julienne: Cut vegetables or meat into strips of varying size.

Deglaze: Dissolve juices caramelized in pot bottoms with a little liquid,

cooking broth, wine, any alcohol, etc., according to the recipe.

Poach: To gently cook in a liquid, uncovered, and without boiling.

Reduce: Simmer a broth or bouillon to lose volume and to gain in flavor

concentration.

Reserve: Put prepared food aside, waiting to put it to use it in the current

recipe. Sometimes, this poses problems. Amateur cooks do not have as

many burners and other equipment at their disposal as their professional

counterparts do. Consider utilizing the oven put on low heat with its door

open, the steamer that enables you to keep food warm in the basket above

the steam, a heat diffuser to slow down the heating capacity of a gas

burner, a brick preheated in the oven, the microwave oven set on lowest power, the heating radiator in winter if you have central heating, or the hearth of your wood burning fireplace.

Soak: To leave an ingredient for a relatively long time in a liquid so that the ingredient picks up the liquid's flavor. When doing this with meat, it is called "marinating."

Thicken: Add an ingredient—flour, butter, cream, egg yolk, starch, etc.—for smoothness.

A minimum of kitchen equipment

None of our recipes require more kitchen equipment than is usual in a typical kitchen. You should certainly have the following handy: blender, immersion blender, food processor, food mill with varying sizes of disks, a chef's knife or cleaver, a fine china cap (that is, a small fine-meshed pointed strainer), a mortar and pestle, cheesecloth with which to line the china cap or strainer when straining liquids, a paring knife, a whisk, a baking sheet or oven tray, and the classic set of stockpot, stewpot, and saucepans of varying sizes. A pressure cooker is not absolutely necessary; it is, however, a time saver. If you use it for meat and vegetable stocks, it will have to be opened while in operation to add the vegetables according to the cooking time they require. By putting it under cold running water while it is locked, it can be opened much faster without the risk of burning yourself.

Last practical advice

When you prepare meat stock, plan for a quantity slightly greater than the one that is required for the meal, let it cool and freeze some in ice cube trays. You will have amazing ready made cooking stocks or sauces.